REDEEMED

Warren Ravenscroft

Redeemed
© **Warren Ravenscroft 2025**

Paperback ISBN: 978-0-646-72560-4

Cover Image: Kevin Carden | Lightstock

Scripture taken from the New King James Spirit Filled Life Bible.
Copyright © 1982 by Thomas Nelson.
Used by permission. All rights reserved.

All rights reserved. No part of this publication may be reproduced, stored in a retrieval system, or transmitted in any form or by any means electronic, mechanical, photocopying, recording, or therwise, without the prior written permission of the author.

Published in Australia by Warren Ravenscroft
www.wittonbooks.com

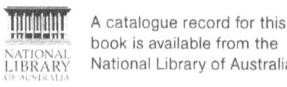

A catalogue record for this book is available from the National Library of Australia

The Lord is my Shepherd;

I shall not want.

He makes me to lie down

in green pastures;

He leads me beside still waters.

He restores my soul;

He leads me in the paths

of righteousness

for His name's sake.

Psalm 23:1–3

CONTENTS

Introduction 7
The Lost Sheep 13
The Lost Coin 29
The Prodigal Son 43
   a) The Son Lost 43
   b) The Lost Redeemed 57
   c) The Self-righteous Brother 70
The Unjust Steward 83
The Law, the Prophets, and the Kingdom 95
Conclusion: The Lost Things 107

Other Lessons 119
   a) Peter 119
   b) Zacchaeus 152
   c) Thomas 165
   d) Cleansed and Restored 177
   e) Jonah 191
   f) Judah 212
   g) Tamar 238
   h) Rahab 248
   i) Ruth 266
   j) Jonah and Peter 283

Song: *I've Been Redeemed* 289

Other Books by the Author 293

INTRODUCTION

Many people in the Bible, both Old and New Testaments, were "Redeemed". Most people are well-known, while others are obscure. Some people in the Old Testament, such as Jonah, Judah, Tamar, Rahab, and Ruth, were chosen for this book.

Those in the New Testament are: Peter, Zacchaeus, Thomas and the Woman with the issue of blood. Four of the Parables Jesus told are also about redemption: The Lost Sheep, The Lost Coin, The Prodigal Son and the Unjust Steward. Luke 15–16

A classic story about Jeremiah and the potter's house is a wonderful example of the way people are "Redeemed" in the Bible. The following verses demonstrate what transpired when Jeremiah was obedient to the word of Father God.

"Arise and go down to the potter's house,
and there I will cause you to hear My words.'

"Then I went down to the potter's house,
and there he was, making something at the wheel.
And the vessel that he made of clay
was marred in the hand of the potter;

so he made it again into another vessel,

and it seemed good to the potter to make."

Jeremiah 18:2–4

When Jeremiah visited the potter's house, he learned the potter rejected some of the pots, maybe because of poor-quality clay. As Father God is sovereign over His people, what He designs is not dependent on the person's response.

Just as the clay can frustrate the potter's intentions and make him alter the vessel, so Father God chooses to change our responses to suit His ordained plan and purpose. As we sometimes ruin the clay in the Father's hands, so He takes what we have done and remoulds us into something fit for His use, although how we turn out may not be what we intended, but all in the design of Father God.

In the parables Jesus told recorded in Luke, the Lost Sheep, the Lost Coin and the Prodigal Son, it would appear Jesus was not only addressing the people of the day, but the Scribes and Pharisees, and two of His disciples, Matthew and James, not Jesus' cousin, who were at odds with each other. Matthew was a Customs Officer, and James was a Zealot, which could prove a recipe for disaster.

Let's focus on Matthew, who was a Jew but worked for the Romans. He represents the prodigal son. *"Wasted his substance"* is an interesting phrase. What is the meaning of *"substance"* in this story? While many focus on physical, this is all spiritual.

So, what did he *"waste"*, which is a better understanding of this word *"prodigal living"*? Daily prayer, going to the Synagogue, listening and taught from those inspired to share the Torah.

He spent time with non-believers rather than like-minded people. After a time, a famine came (Luke 15:14), and he found himself in a spiritual desert. Matthew is sitting at the receipt of customs, and Jesus showed up and said, *"Follow Me."* Matthew closed his books and followed Jesus.

Matthew did not need to reconcile his bookkeeping. Everything was in order so he could, at any time, close the books and walk away, leaving a true and accurate account for the one to follow. In the story of the Prodigal Son, Jesus shared:

> *"He would gladly have filled his stomach with pods."*
>
> Luke 15:16a

Let's focus on James. James became a Zealot with a flaming patriotism and an embittered hatred for all who compromised with Rome. He would kill Matthew in an instant, as he was top of the list for assassination.

As James stood with his Zealot companions, did they ask embarrassing questions as to why Matthew was considered worthy to be with them? This was the obvious thinking of the Scribes and Pharisees, those who thought they were keeping the law meticulously.

As Jesus shared the parables, each disciple was scrutinising his life and their past actions. Did they line up with the teaching of Jesus, or did they need to make some adjustments to their thinking? This was a double-barreled approach by Jesus, as the Scribes and Pharisees were also targets.

Jesus was teaching about redemption and the cost involved for the individual. At other times, those who sought forgiveness and put their faith in Jesus were rewarded.

Those covered in the Old Testament — Jonah, Judah, Tamah, Rahab, and Ruth — had their own redemption path to walk, under the leading and guiding of the Lord. Through obedience, although the way was often obscured, each found a way through the darkness to a bright new day and future.

Jeremiah went down to the potter's house, where he observed each piece fashioned, but some were defective. Not until the pottery was shaped to the potter's plan was the pottery ready for the kiln, then fired and became a useful item, crafted by the master craftsman.

Each person passed through their own refining fire to be "Redeemed". Each had a journey allotted to them; some were victorious, while others bore battle scars.

We all have a path to walk through the fires of life. When our life's tested by the *"Refiner's fire"*, what's left is our gift to Father God.

Introduction

"For no other foundation can anyone lay
than that which is laid,
which is Jesus Christ.
Now if anyone builds on this foundation
with gold, silver, precious stones, wood,
hay, straw, each one's work will become clear;
for the Day will declare it,
because it will be revealed by fire;
and the fire will test each one's work,
of what sort it is.
If anyone's work which he has built on it endures,
he will receive a reward.
If anyone's work is burned,
he will suffer loss;
but he himself will be saved,
yet so as through fire."

1 Corinthians 3:11–15

This text explores the theme of "Redemption" as seen in various Bible stories, comparing Old and New Testament examples, using parables and character studies to highlight spiritual transformation.

- **Old Testament examples:** Jonah, Judah, Tamar, Rahab, and Ruth all undergo journeys of redemption through obedience and faith.
- **New Testament characters:** Peter, Zacchaeus, Thomas, and the Woman with the issue of blood are referenced as redeemed.
- **Parables about Redemption:** The Lost Sheep, The Lost Coin, The Prodigal Son, and the Unjust Steward illustrate God's pursuit and transformation of lost individuals. Luke 15–16
- **Jeremiah and the potter's house:** Symbolises God's reshaping of individuals according to their response and willingness to change.
- **Focus on Matthew and James:** Highlights their contrasting backgrounds (tax collector vs. zealot) and underscores Jesus' call to redemption.
- **Parables:** Addressed both followers and critics, urging personal reflection and adjustment.
- **Key message:** Redemption requires faith, obedience, self-examination, and sometimes enduring hardship through the *"Refiner's fire"*.

THE LOST SHEEP

"What man of you, having a hundred sheep,
if he loses one of them,
does not leave the ninety-nine in the wilderness,
and go after the one which is lost until he finds it?
And when he has found it, he lays it on his shoulders, rejoicing.

And when he comes home,
he calls together his friends and neighbours, saying to them,
'Rejoice with me, for I have found my sheep which was lost!'
I say to you that likewise there will be more joy in heaven
over one sinner who repents than over
ninety-nine just persons who need no repentance."

Luke 15:1–7

Jesus was travelling to Jerusalem and gathered a large following of people eager to hear His teaching. He told three parables (Luke 15:4–32) to the Pharisees, scribes, tax collectors, sinners and a fourth parable (Luke 16:1–13) to the disciples.

The first parable is the "Lost Sheep". This parable is about a shepherd who noticed one of the sheep in his care was missing. He secured the others in the pen, then set off to find the lost sheep. Having found the sheep, he laid it on his shoulders, carried it home, and everyone was happy about this outcome.

As we examine the parable a little more in-depth, a deeper meaning surfaces. Under the watchful eye of this shepherd, perhaps the sheep wanders off because it's looking for grass in the sparseness of this arid place. In other words, the sheep is not content with what's provided.

Some other shepherds who are not watchful have no thought for those strayed sheep, but let them go to find their own fate. The shepherd thinks, "These sheep have wandered off, so they can deal with the mess they will end up with."

The good shepherd, although watchful, enables the sheep to wander, noting the direction the sheep is heading. He is mindful and knows sheep who stray are considered stupid creatures because they have no means of protecting themselves against predators, and will not make their way back to the main group. They will keep on wandering.

Sheep wander for several reasons. They may be following other sheep or become curious about something they see. Other undernourished grass and water appeal to them rather than the grass provided for their needs. The prophet Isaiah understood sheep, for he likened them to people who were prone to wander when he wrote:

The Lost Sheep

"All we like sheep have gone astray;
We have turned, everyone,
to his own way."

Isaiah 53:6a

The good shepherd eventually does a head count, and because he has an intimate relationship with each sheep, as they all have names, he is aware of which sheep is missing. One sheep out of the hundred he cares for is missing. Does he quietly think to himself, "Not again! How stubborn is this sheep?"

The good shepherd could head off in any direction, but because he is very aware of the way the sheep was heading, he walked in that direction. As the shepherd surveys the vast countryside, the sheep is not in sight, but he persists and eventually noticed a sheep lying helplessly on the ground in the distance.

The sheep can do nothing for itself as it has become *"cast down"* (John 15:5). The meaning of *"cast down"* is the sheep became tired, found a nice place to rest then lies down. This could occur because the woollen fleece is too heavy, weighed down with dirt, or the sheep devoured too much food. The sheep simply can't go any further.

The real problem arises when the sheep wants to get back on its feet, and can't, as the weight prevents it from rolling over and standing on its unsupportive legs. Panic sets in as the sheep struggles, which only paralyses its legs, adding further complications to its situation. Now helpless, the sheep is at the mercy of any passing predator, including wild dogs, other animals and birds of prey.

The good shepherd understands time is of the essence, as in the hot sun, the sheep will die if unattended. The shepherd runs to the sheep and immediately helps to turn the sheep over. "Can the sheep stand on its own?" is a question to be answered before he continues.

As the sheep is completely helpless, the shepherd massages the muscles of the legs to renew circulation of the blood, gently supporting the sheep, not only physically but with words of comfort, not ridicule. Slowly but surely, the sheep responds to the good shepherd and stands on its own, but this is only short-lived, as the sheep once more stumbles and falls as it tries to walk.

Unable to walk, the shepherd laid the sheep on his shoulders and carried it home. As the flock most likely belongs to the community, any loss is felt while reinstatement is cause for celebration. Does this say anything to us about how we should act and care for those in our fellowship?

This parable was shared by Jesus with the men in the group, as they were shepherds, assuring them, Father God was interested in them and seeking the lost, to help and return them to the fold. Everyone understood the significance of caring for sheep, even if they had little comprehension of the spiritual meaning of the parable.

Most, if not all, were acquainted with the Psalms, read in their synagogues. The sons of Korah used the words *"cast down"* in two of their psalms, verse after verse.

> *"As the deer pants for the water brooks,*
> *so pants my soul for You, O God.*
> *My soul thirsts for God,*
> *for the living God.*
> *Why are you cast down, O my soul?*
> *O my God,*
> *my soul is cast down within me.*
> *Why are you cast down, O my soul?"*
>
> Psalm 42, selected verses

> *"Why are you cast down, O my soul?*
> *And why are you disquieted within me?*
> *Hope in God;*
> *for I shall yet praise Him,*
> *the help of my countenance and my God."*
>
> Psalm 43:5

What the psalmist is saying, while Israel is similar to a *"cast-down"* sheep, disquieted, experiencing a feeling of concern or unease, they look forward to the day when, although they appear to be helpless now, Father God will rescue them from their predators, those who would do them harm.

Another psalm the crowd could recall was a psalm of David, who shared and wrote:

> *"The Lord is my Shepherd;*
> *I shall not want.*
> *He makes me to lie down*
> *in green pastures;*
> *He leads me beside still waters.*
> *He restores my soul;*
> *He leads me in the paths*
> *of righteousness*
> *for His name's sake.*
>
> Psalm 23:1–3

The gentle process by which a shepherd *"restores"* a *"cast-down"* sheep back to its feet, is meant by the brief phrase, *"He restores my soul"* (Psalm 23:3). It's a beautiful picture of the intimate, compassionate relationship between the Good Shepherd and His sheep.

Some sheep are stubborn, always wanting to do things their way, unaware they need to follow the directions of the shepherd. After all, they are sheep. David has some further words for those who present stubbornness as an attribute.

The Lost Sheep

> *"Yea, though I walk through the valley*
> *of the shadow of death, I will fear no evil;*
> *for You are with me;*
> *Your rod and Your staff, they comfort me."*
>
> Psalm 23:4

The stubbornness of a sheep has caused it to stray into uncharted waters, now helpless, *"cast down"*, awaiting its fate. While some remain defiant, others cry out to Father God and rely on Him to rescue them as they say, *"for You are with me"*. It is never good to put Father God to the test of rescuing you from the situation you blatantly put yourself in. Jesus said:

> *It is written again,*
> *"You shall not tempt the Lord your God."*
>
> Matthew 4:7

David referred to the shepherd using a rod and staff to comfort the sheep, to guide, not punish, to chase predators away. A stubborn sheep that continued to wander off or pursue its own way may need a rod of correction to keep it safe. This is for the stubborn sheep's protection and safety. It may at times not be pleasant for the strayed sheep, but certainly necessary.

The writer to the Hebrews explains the *"Rod"* to the congregation of his day when he wrote:

> *"My son, do not despise*
> *the discipline of the Lord,*
> *Nor be discouraged when you are rebuked by Him;*
> *for whom the Lord loves He disciplines,*
> *and scourges every son whom He receives."*
>
> Hebrews 12:5–6

It is easy for a believer to become *"cast down"* if or when prayer and reading, studying the Word of God, is a secondary thing, not done each day. When we petition daily for His care and guidance, He assures each one we're not walking alone, but walking in the foreordained steps of Father God. His mercy and grace will cover every situation we are called to face.

Father God promised to be with us in all situations. As a child of the Father, we are confident in His word:

> *"I will never leave you nor forsake you.*
> *The Lord is my helper;*
> *I will not fear.*
> *What can man do to me?"*
>
> Hebrews 13:5b–6

It is not enough to look at the past and cling to past grace; we must actively trust Father God, who continues to provide what is needed every moment of the day. We need to remember, it is only through repentance, humility, and Father God's grace, we are made right from being *"cast down"* in the all-sufficiency of Father God's love.

Jesus shared this parable to bring new understanding to the God of the Old Testament, from One to be feared, to One who loved and cared for His people. Father God still loves and cares for all as He seeks the lost, carrying them if necessary, the *"cast-down"* back to Himself and into the flock.

Horatio Richmond Palmer (1834–1907) understood the message contained in Jesus' parable of the "Lost Sheep," which he shared with the crowd. I would share with you the following verses of a song he wrote.

> *Yield not to temptation,*
> *for yielding is sin.*
> *Each vict'ry will help you*
> *some other to win.*
> *Fight valiantly onward;*
> *dark passions subdue.*
> *Look ever to Jesus;*
> *He'll carry you through.*

Refrain:
> *Ask the Saviour to help you,*
> *comfort, strengthen, and keep you.*
> *He is willing to aid you;*
> *He will carry you through.*

Shun evil companions;
bad language disdain.
God's name hold in rev'rence,
nor take it in vain.
Be thoughtful and earnest,
kind-hearted and true.
Look ever to Jesus;
He'll carry you through. [Refrain]

To him that o'ercometh
God giveth a crown.
Through faith we will conquer,
though often cast down.
He who is our Saviour
our strength will renew.
Look ever to Jesus;
He'll carry you through. [Refrain]

Public Domain

Overview

- The parable of the Lost Sheep teaches about the shepherd's care for his flock.
- It symbolises Father God's love and pursuit of those who stray.

The Lost Sheep

The Parable

- A shepherd has 100 sheep and loses one.
- He leaves the 99 to search for the lost one.
- Upon finding it, he rejoices and celebrates with friends.

Key Themes

- Watchfulness of the Shepherd
- The shepherd is attentive to each sheep's needs.
- He knows when one is missing.
- Reasons for Wandering
- Sheep may stray due to curiosity or seeking better grass.
- They cannot return on their own.
- How sheep become *"Cast Down"*.
- A sheep can become helpless and panic when it cannot rise.
- The shepherd acts quickly to rescue the sheep.

Relationship with Father God

- The parable reflects Father God's desire to restore those who are lost.
- It highlights the intimate relationship between Father God and His people.

Biblical References

- Isaiah 53:6 compares people to wandering sheep.
- Psalms express feelings of being "cast down" and the longing for Father God's help.

Conclusion

- The shepherd's actions illustrate Father God's compassion and care.
- The parable encourages believers to trust in Father God for guidance and support.

The Lost Sheep

Aussie Version

"Gidday mate."
"Gidday Yeshua. Howya goin?"
"Seems like oneofdem jolly jumbucks ave gon misssin."
"Fairdimkum. Doyah know where?"
"Na'hr mate. Just ganna go and hava look."
"Doyah wanna take blue wiv ya?"
"Na'hr. He'll only get in duh way. Quicker omah ohm."
"Alright mate. Be careful. I'll look afta dees ov'er jumbucks foryah. I'll takem down to dah billabong fora drink."
"Goodo mate."

"Hey, Yeshua!"
"Yea'r mate."
"We're havin a barbie later. Wanna join us? I can throw an extra coupla prawns on for yah."
"Sounds good mate. See yah."

Having left the jumbucks and lambs in a secure paddock under the watchful eyes of His mates, Yeshua made His way back out over the vast area before Him. Hills dotted the plains stretched out before him, with some trees and billabongs marking good places for shade, grass and water.

His Akubra proved an invaluable friend from the heat of the day. With each passing moment, Yeshua knew death drew nearer and nearer for the one He was looking for.

As Yeshua looked tediously for the jumbuck, a few inquisitive kangaroos and wallabies hopped past, along with the odd emu.

The slight breeze suddenly changed direction. As Yeshua paused to listen, He thought He heard a slight bleat. He strained to tell which way the sound came from.

Oh no! Muffling the bleat were the sounds of running wild dogs. Yeshua picked up his pace, running in the direction of the bleating sound. Using his stock whip, he managed to scare away the pack of wild dogs who were startled at His appearance.

Yeshua came to where the jumbuck was lying. He knelt beside this exhausted jumbuck, providing it with some much-needed shade from the hot noonday sun. Yeshua noticed the sheep had found a lovely divot in the ground and made itself comfortable, lying down, finding some relief from the heavy load of wool it was carrying.

Bending over the jumbuck, Yeshua gently massaged its legs, as they were paralysed from the lack of circulation of blood through its struggle to get to its feet again. Yeshua had seen this so many times before, a cast-down sheep. Most never survived, ravaged by wild dogs, other predators, or birds of prey.

Yeshua took great care in lifting the sheep onto His shoulders, now making the arduous task of walking back to the paddock and safety.

As Yeshua came within eyeshot of the other jumbucks, He could hear them bleating for joy. His mates also noticed the noise of the jumbucks, dropped what they were doing and ran to help Yeshua.

"Hey, Mate. Wanna hand?"
"Yeah mate, that'd be great", replied Yeshua.
"Arr mate. Werdidja finda?" one of the drovers asked.
"Out parst da old billabong. Must hav thought she new bettar dan us. Safe now. Dah dogs almost hader. I rived justintime. Good fortune I callit."
"Hey, Yeshua."
"Yea'r mate."
"Yahr justintime. Grab a plate n join the rest of vus."
"Thanks, mate. Bin a long day, but worf it."

THE LOST COIN

"Or what woman, having ten silver coins,
if she loses one coin, does not light a lamp,
sweep the house,
and search carefully until she finds it?

And when she has found it,
she calls her friends and neighbours together,
saying, 'Rejoice with me,
for I have found the piece which I lost!'

Likewise, I say to you,
there is joy in the presence of the angels of God
over one sinner who repents."

Luke 15:8–10

Jesus continued teaching with the parable of the "Lost Coin". This appeared to be about a woman who lost one of her coins, lit a lamp, then swept the floor until she found the coin, and returned it to the others. Everyone is happy with this outcome. Jesus could have chosen this parable as He focused on the women in the crowd.

Again, a deeper meaning is contained within this parable. These ten coins were very significant for all married women. The mark of a married woman was a head-dress made of ten silver coins linked together by a silver chain called a "Semedi".

The "Semedi" was equivalent to a wedding ring. This could not be taken from her for debt, such was its importance. A small item could easily become consumed in the floor covering used at this time. She would be very emotional finding this loss, and sweeping the floor was painstaking, to say the least. Such was the effort to locate and restore the lost to its rightful place. Does this reflect our diligence towards those in our care?

Jesus' message was about the lost. Those who were tax collectors, sinners, women, the scribes and Pharisees were all present, a very mixed audience. Those who strayed for any reason, needed to be found and restored to their rightful place, as acceptance of past failings was required to be forgiven and forgotten.

Jesus was saying, the God they worshipped accepted wayward people who returned to Father God's family, and truly repented for the situations and sins of the past. Once they saw their need, they were to be welcomed back and become part of the fellowship, no questions asked.

Do you think James was hearing this message? I wonder how his thoughts were changed toward the tax collector in the group of disciples? The scribes and Pharisees were becoming more agitated with every passing parable, but Jesus had a lesson to share with them all.

I believe it would be profitable for us to stop here and process what has been taught by Jesus so far. What was Jesus telling His listeners about those who had strayed? What was He saying about finding these people? What was the attitude to be when they had seen their waywardness and returned?

As I meditated on the deeper meaning of the parable, it appeared to be a little overwhelming as what is expected of us each concerning those who not only left the fold, but in going after, locating, and applying the balm of understanding, to obtain healing.

Encouragement and support, caring for them if necessary, bringing them to a place of safety, content once more to be with like-minded, strengthening people. Am I up for this, or does it appear to be too hard? Do I care for these people like the woman who had the coins? While I would choose to be numbered with Jesus and the disciples, I think my place may be with the scribes and Pharisees.

While the day of grace is still with us, does the urgency of these lost souls impact us to the point of actually doing something? Has the hectic lifestyle we lead somewhat dulled our enthusiasm for the lost? Is it all about convenience when looking at this role we are called to fulfil?

Maybe the real message for us is being obedient to the promptings and listening to what the Holy Spirit asks us to do, but then, as we follow the lead of the Shepherd, sometimes the way back for some is too hard, as they prefer the lifestyle they have become accustomed to.

A scripture verse comes to mind which says,

> *"Unless the Lord builds the house,*
> *they labour in vain who build it."*
>
> Psalm 127:1a

Just like the sower (Matthew 13:3–9, 18–23). Unless our Lord has prepared the ground, no matter what we do or say, our labour will produce nothing, maybe harden the ground further. This type of failure could also lead to us being discouraged as well.

The parable of the "Lost Coin" is about the third person in the Trinity, the Holy Spirit. Because we are living after Pentecost, the message of this parable has much more significance for us.

The Lost Coin:
Represents a person who is separated from Father God, perhaps through sin or a wandering away from faith.

The Woman:
Symbolises the Holy Spirit's persistent love and pursuit of those who are lost.

The Search:
Depicts Father God's active effort to seek out and redeem those who are separated from Him.

The Rejoicing:
Illustrates the joy in heaven when a sinner repents and returns to Father God.

This headpiece, the "Semedi", was given to the betrothed on her wedding day by her husband. Although given to her, the headpiece still belonged to her husband, as did she. This was similar to a wedding ring, and she had the responsibility of looking after this gift. The "Semedi" could not be taken away from her to pay a debt. It is thought some husbands gave more to their wives, so when the tax collector or customs officer called, or a debt was to be paid, this "Semedi" was exempt. How shrewd is this?

As the "Semedi" were a gift from her betrothed, signifying she was in a time of marriage, they were precious to the wife. When a marriage was agreed upon by both people, the groom's family would pay for the bride, similar to bride-price, which still happens in Papua New Guinea. She was bought at a price.

Paul, when writing his first letter to the Corinthians, said,

> *"For you were bought at a price;*
> *therefore glorify God in your body*
> *and in your spirit,*
> *which are God's."*

1Corinthians 6:20

Jesus was crucified to pay the penalty for our sin, and for us to receive forgiveness, it cost Father God His Son's life. We were *bought at a price*. I remember Jacob worked seven years to secure his marriage to Rachael, only to have Leah substituted by her father, Laban. Jacob was then required to work another seven years for Rachael. Genesis 29:18–30

Having experienced Salvation, we now belong to Father God and are accepted into His family as one of His children. As the amount was agreed upon, and Father God paid the price, we now belong to Him.

The woman was prompted to take a lamp, as this would make the lost article easier to find on the darkened floor. Maybe the dirt had cracks in it or was just loose dirt? Whatever the condition of the floor, light would expel the darkness, and as she swept, the lost coin should be seen.

Jesus was saying to this mixed crowd, as well as His disciples and especially to the women who followed Jesus and supported His ministry, that only through Him would the true light be revealed. What Jesus had used as a story was one that appealed to His women followers, as they all understood about a clean house.

As we look at the parable, I noticed the woman knew exactly where she had lost the coin. It was in the house where she lived. Not outside, not down the road, at the shops, at a friend's place, but in her home. Where is our spiritual home? We're not always ready for the unexpected, especially when it is in our spiritual home. Our spiritual home is guarded by the Holy Spirit. It is He who takes our prayers to Father God on our behalf, interpreting our needs much better than we can.

As I meditated on the ten coins, what did they represent to me? I was given ten things.

1. Faith. Romans 10:17
2. Hope. Proverbs 13:12
3. Love. 1 John 4:16
4. Trust. Proverbs 3:5-6
5. Peace. John 14:27
6. Security. Psalm 91:1
7. Wisdom. James 1:5
8. Understanding. Proverbs 3:13
9. Provision. 2 Corinthians 9:8
10. Eternal Life. John 10:28

How many of these do we take for granted as we live in the secret place of the Most High? As we take refuge under His wings? (Psalm 91:1–16). Do you know how precious you are to Father God? He formed you, redeemed you, calls you by name and protects and comforts you. You are precious in His sight; honoured and loved for all eternity.

> *"Since you are precious in My sight,*
>
> *you have been honoured,*
>
> *and I have loved you."*

Isaiah 43:4a

As we belong to Father God, we are His, so He sends the Holy Spirit to guide us in the way we should walk. Father God has also given us free will to choose between prompting and what we regard as best. While the woman knew where she had lost the coin, she was unaware of how the coin had become lost. Was it carelessness? Was it neglect for not repairing the thread that held the coin in place?

The Bible tells us:

> *"The thief does not come*
> *except to steal, and to kill,*
> *and to destroy."*
>
> John 10:10a

Did we somehow allow the evil ones to enter our spiritual home and cause havoc? How many become complacent in their spiritual life, spiritually dead and not aware? How many have ceased searching for the elusive lost coin, which now appeared to be gone forever? How many have gone past the point of no return?

The Holy Spirit continues to prompt us every step of our lives. When John wrote to the church in Philadelphia, he had the following words of warning for this persevering congregation:

> *"Hold fast what you have,*
> *that no one steal your crown."*
>
> Revelation 3:11b

As I meditate on the previous ten things given, what one, if lost, would I grieve for the most? I guess it would be different for each of us. Which one would you not want to lose, unable to be sure you would find it amongst the rubbish, the dirt? For me, while I can't imagine wanting to be without any one of them, to lose "Eternal Life" would be disastrous.

To know and realise I would spend eternity in the Lake of Fire with the evil powers, and all things evil, is too much for me to comprehend, yet many are choosing, not concerned with their fate. The goats in the church are in for a shock when the books are opened and the shed blood of Jesus has been trampled on and discarded. Hebrews 10:29

Ten Gifts from Father God

As I reflected on the coins previously given, I contemplated ten other coins that are available for those who have been chosen and called by Father God.

1. Grace. Ephesians 2:8-9
2. Repentance. 1 John 1:9
3. Forgiveness. James 5:16
4. Redemption. Psalm 103:12
5. Salvation. Acts 4:12
6. Sealed. Ephesians 1:13-14
7. Justification. Romans 3:24-26
8. Sanctification. 1 Corinthians 6:11
9. Glorification. Colossians 3:4
10. Eternal Life. John 5:24

Grace:

Father God's unmerited favour and love, offered freely to all humanity. This Grace is the foundation for Salvation, making it possible for sinful humans to be reconciled to Father God.

Repentance:

A turning away from sin and towards Father God. It involves acknowledging one's sinfulness and a desire to change one's life in accordance with Father God's will.

Forgiveness:

Pardoning an offence, releasing the offender from the consequences of their actions, and letting go of resentment or the desire for retribution.

Redemption:

The act of being saved from sin, its consequences, and spiritual bondage through the costly sacrifice of Jesus Christ.

Salvation:

Rescued from the consequences of sin, which include separation from Father God and spiritual death, is achieved through faith in Jesus Christ.

Sealed:

Sealed often refers to the Holy Spirit's work in believers, signifying ownership, protection, and validation of their relationship with Father God.

Justification:
Father God's act of declaring a sinner Righteous in His sight through faith in His Son. Justification can't be earned through good works, but forgiveness and acceptance by Father God based on Christ's sacrifice.

Sanctification:
Sanctification refers to the process of being set apart for Father God's purposes. This is a lifelong journey of transformation where believers grow in Grace and become more like Christ.

Glorification:
This is the final stage of Salvation, where believers are transformed into the perfect likeness of Jesus Christ, both in body, soul and spirit.

Eternal Life:
A state of unending life with Father God, often described as a gift received through faith in Jesus Christ. This life is characterised by spiritual transformation and fellowship with Father God.

In Christian theology, Salvation, or entrance into Eternal Life, is often described as a process beginning with Father God's Grace and culminating in a transformed life through Faith in Jesus Christ. This journey involves receiving Father God's free gift of "Grace", which enables Repentance and Faith, ultimately leading to the free gift of "Eternal Life".

Progression:

The journey from "Grace" to "Eternal Life" is not a one-time event but an ongoing process of growth and transformation. It involves ongoing reliance on Father God's grace, continuing faith, and a commitment to living a life that reflects Christ's teachings.

The parable emphasises Father God's value of every *"Called"* individual, as there is great rejoicing in heaven when someone follows the promptings of the Holy Spirit and turns back to Father God. It highlights Father God's love and compassion for all, even those considered "lost" or less fortunate by the church.

Jesus is gently leading James the Zealot in his thoughts towards Matthew the Tax Collector. Both are hearing what Jesus is saying. Will reconciliation come to both these disciples? Jesus hasn't finished with either of them, as He continued to mould their thinking and bias one toward the other.

Overview

- The parable of the Lost Coin illustrates Father God's love for the lost and the joy of repentance.
- It highlights the importance of seeking and restoring those who stray from faith.

Key Themes

- The Lost Coin: Represents individuals separated from Father God due to sin or straying.
- The Woman: Symbolises the Holy Spirit's persistent love and pursuit.
- The Search: Depicts Father God's active effort to redeem those lost.
- The Rejoicing: Illustrates joy in heaven when a sinner repents.

Cultural Context

- The ten coins were significant in marriage, akin to a wedding ring.
- The loss of a coin would be emotional and significant, reflecting the importance of the search.

Spiritual Reflection

- Encouragement to care for those who have strayed.
- The urgency of seeking the lost amidst life's distractions.

The Role of the Holy Spirit

- The Holy Spirit guides and prompts believers in their spiritual journey.
- Each coin represents spiritual gifts that should not be taken for granted.

Gifts from Father God

- Grace: Unmerited favour for Salvation.
- Repentance: Acknowledgment of sin and turning back to God.
- Forgiveness: Releasing resentment.
- Redemption: Saved from sin through Jesus' sacrifice.
- Eternal Life: The ultimate gift received through faith.

THE PRODIGAL SON

The Son Lost

A certain man had two sons.
And the younger of them said to his father,
"Father, give me the portion of goods that falls to me."
So he divided to them his livelihood.
And not many days after,
the younger son gathered all together,
journeyed to a far country,
and there wasted his possessions with prodigal living.

But when he had spent all,
there arose a severe famine in that land,
and he began to be in want.
Then he went and joined himself to a citizen of that country,
and he sent him into his fields to feed swine.
And he would gladly have filled his stomach
with the pods that the swine ate,
and no one gave him anything.

But when he came to himself, he said,
"How many of my father's hired servants
have bread enough and to spare, and I perish with hunger!
I will arise and go to my father, and will say to him,
'Father, I have sinned against heaven and before you,
and I am no longer worthy to be called your son.
Make me like one of your hired servants'."
And he arose and came to his father.

But when he was still a great way off,
his father saw him and had compassion,
and ran and fell on his neck and kissed him.
And the son said to him,
"Father, I have sinned against heaven and in your sight,
and am no longer worthy to be called your son."

Luke 15:11-21

Jesus continued with His teaching. Hard on the heels of the "Lost Sheep" and the "Lost Coin" comes the parable of "The Prodigal Son". While we have read these three parables and received much teaching about them, I wondered how those listening to Jesus accepted what He was teaching in relation to their culture or way of life. While the scribes and Pharisees criticised, the tax collectors and sinners pressed forward to hear the words Jesus taught.

Jesus now focused on the parable of "The Prodigal Son". When rereading this parable, it became obvious that there is more than one prodigal son, and then there is the father. Jesus knew His audience contained all three. There were the parents who were concerned for their children. The children who appeared to be doing all things right, and then there were the rebellious ones.

Does this still happen today? Some people do nothing but criticise instead of getting alongside and encouraging, tearing down, not building up, because the person did not fit into their expectations and beliefs. As I replay my teenage years, tears come to my eyes as the best-intentioned saints often created a load far too heavy for some of the younger converts to bear.

The younger son came to his father and demanded his portion of the inheritance (Luke 15:12). The rebellious son was saying, "I wish you were dead!" This would not have happened in an instant, but was building up for some time. If he were like any other son, he would be rebelling against the legalistic side of religion. He'd had enough.

Perhaps the older brother's attitude to his younger sibling was responsible for his decision to leave the family home. Was the older brother always taking charge, telling him what to do and finding fault? Do as I say, not as I do? I'm in charge?

Harassment by other family members was nothing new. The first was Abel harassed by Cain over Abel's offering to Father God accepted, and his was not. Genesis 4:8

A second was Esau and Jacob (Genesis 27:41). A third was Joseph and his brothers (Genesis 37:27). A fourth is when David visits his brothers, as they were fighting the Philistines, who accused David of pride and insolence of heart, to which David replied:

"What have I done now?

Is there not a cause?"

1 Samuel 17:29

The younger brother just wanted out, like so many people today. He wanted to remove himself from this whole situation, to find freedom, do his own thing without answering to anyone. Maybe he was hoping someone would just appreciate what he did?

As agricultural land was scarce, those who worked on the land never lived on their farmland because they didn't want to waste good farm land by building on it. Instead, people lived in small, compact villages called "Insulas" or a block of buildings clustered around a central courtyard, where extended families would live, work and interact. From here, they went out to work on their farms.

These Insulas were made up of family members and close relatives, and everyone knew each other well. Children grew up around their grandparents, aunts, uncles, and cousins, as well as other neighbours. To understand this story in the proper context, we need to recognise, the conversation between the younger son and his father took place in front of a watching community of family, relatives, and neighbours.

As the younger son contemplated what his options were, he knew if he failed after leaving, he faced ridicule and rejection from his family as well as the community when or if he returned. This was called the "Kezazah", or a ceremony, a Jewish village would carry out in exactly this situation, where someone had left home, rejected the community's principles, lost all his or her possessions to the Gentiles, and then chosen to return.

With this in mind, the younger son went to a far country, to live with the Gentiles, unbelievers. By doing this, he was out from under the law and legalistic religion weighing him down. A young person with no living skills was a recipe for disaster from the beginning. He was taken advantage of by the people in the world. Has anything changed?

When the younger brother returned, the older brother had much to say in condemning his actions while away. How did he know or presume what his little brother was up to? This says a lot about what happened before the younger son left. He might have been a rebellious child, but he was given teachings in his childhood he adhered to.

I personally think the prodigal didn't commit the things his brother accused him of. To substantiate this claim, I would refer to a verse in the parable.

> *"And he would gladly have filled his stomach*
> *with the pods that the swine ate,*
> *and no one gave him anything."*

Luke 15:16

He could have, he thought about it, but he didn't. He was suffering extreme hunger, but he didn't steal from his employer to satisfy his need.

How easy is it to justify those things wrong in the sight of Father God? I remember being told even a thief can justify why they steal. If the prodigal couldn't commit this act of stealing in secret, the owner certainly not knowing, then I ask you, how would he have ever slept with prostitutes in front of his acquaintances?

While the prodigal dug his heels in, eventually *"he came to himself"* (v17a). How many people have we grown up with, sat next to in Sunday School, Church, Youth Group, left for whatever reason, never came to themselves? I thank Father God; some have returned.

The question to be addressed is, what does *"he came to himself"* mean? As the prodigal son began to reflect on his miserable condition, or *"he came to his senses"* (Luke 15:17), he realised even his father's servants had it better, as his painful circumstances helped him to see his father in a new light. Hope began to dawn in his heart as he recognised the Holy Spirit's prompting. Psalm 147:11; Isaiah 40:30–31; 1 Timothy 4:10

The Prodigal Son

"He came to himself" suggests the son was previously living in a kind of self-deception or delusion, indulging his desires without considering the consequences. His *"coming to himself"* was a wake-up call, a realisation of his true state and the foolishness of his choices.

This young prodigal returned, but still, it was on his terms. He didn't want to be bound by the restraints he had previously endured. He was at ease being a hired servant. He would be cared for and have some independence. Food, lodging and a paid job, but he needed to accept he would be lorded over by the older brother. Guess this was a small price to pay for security and independence.

Had he forgotten about the "Kezazah Ceremony"? Maybe he realised he would need to go through this humiliation, be rejected by the community, not be part of the family, but be a hired servant. As he pondered his options, where he was, did he have an alternative?

When the prodigal returned home, the father had compassion, ran and embraced his younger son (v20b). The father's love and desire to bless his son never changed, even though the son had left. The father saw the boy returning while he was still some distance away, which meant the father was looking for him. Was there a motive the father required to put into place before his wayward son came into the village?

What did the Kezazeh Ceremony involve? The villagers would break a piece of pottery at the feet of the individual, symbolising they were no longer in the community; they were breaking relations with him. It was a way of shaming the individual, of making him feel completely empty. One thing to note, the ceremony would take place on the outskirts of the village before the individual could make their way back home.

Jewish tradition maintained it was not proper for a Jew over thirty years of age to run; however, the father ran to embrace His son. An older man, especially the head of a wealthy household, would never run, as to do so would be shockingly undignified. To run, a man would need to take the long robe he was wearing and tie it up above the knees. This done, his legs would be exposed, making him look utterly shameful.

What we note here is this father figure symbolises "Royalty", who takes his robe and ties it up, and runs through the village to the outskirts, exposing the nakedness of his legs and shaming himself for the sake of embracing his son. Did the father give any thought to his dignity? He could not!

The father demonstrated to his community the depth of grace, love and forgiveness, as he ran before any of the extended family could break a clay pot at his son's feet. There is no greater dignity than a father running to meet his boy. Isn't this how Father God deals with us when we accept the Holy Spirit's prompting to return and come back to Him?

Now standing in the presence of his father, this dirty, smelly, ragged, shoeless son is embraced by his father. How many barriers have been broken down? So, the son made his confession. *"Father, I have sinned against heaven and in your sight, and am no longer worthy to be called your son"* (v21). He never finished what he intended to say.

This now poses the question: what was his sin? We need to go back to the Old Testament for the answer. *"Honour your father and your mother"* (Exodus 20:12a). He sinned against Father God by breaking His commandment and in the presence of his father. In front of the whole community, he made his wishes known, never expecting the consequences to follow.

Many in the crowd knew exactly what Jesus was saying and heard a message suited for them. Some would shrug it off, totally ignoring what was said, but maybe some people, feeling the pressure of family and religion far too hard, took heart from the words Jesus shared. It was all about the lost. Lost sheep. Lost Coin. Lost Eternal Inheritance.

While meditating on the Prodigal Son, when he *"came to his senses"*, I wondered if he remembered the words written in the book of Proverbs, which said:

> *"Hope deferred makes the heart sick,*
> *but when the desire comes,*
> *it is a tree of life."*

Proverbs 13:12

His hope was in his father accepting him back, not as a son but as a servant. He could have stayed where he was and died physically, but the desire came, and he returned home to find his *"hope"* became a *"tree of life"*. Does this speak to you about where you are at this time and the situations you find yourself in? This is all about our obedience to what the Holy Spirit reveals to us. I am also prompted to think of another passage of scripture which says:

> *"Esau, who for one morsel of food*
> *sold his birthright.*
> *For you know that afterward,*
> *when he wanted to inherit the blessing,*
> *he was rejected,*
> *for he found no place for repentance,*
> *though he sought it diligently with tears."*
>
> Hebrews 12:16b–17

The day of *"grace"* is still available to those who choose to take it. Father God had previously said:

> *"My Spirit shall not strive*
> *with man forever."*
>
> Genesis 6:3a

Many have made their way back under the prompting of the Holy Spirit, who are embraced by Father God, have sought forgiveness, been restored to a child of Father God and obtained Salvation. Father God then clothed them in spiritual clothes of Justification, Sealed, Redemption, Sanctification, and Glorification, which included Eternal Life.

Unfortunately, when the redeemed have returned to where they were, the church they attended, while Father God accepted, people have long memories and often reject the child of Father God, just like the older brother who wanted justice served, not respecting the father's wishes.

As we have shared this journey of forgiveness and reconciliation, I am prompted to share the words of a Psalm of David when he wrote,

> *"One thing I have desired of the Lord,*
> *that will I seek:*
> *That I may dwell in the house of the Lord*
> *all the days of my life,*
> *to behold the beauty of the Lord,*
> *and to enquire in His temple,*
> *for in the time of trouble*
> *He shall hide me in His pavilion;*
> *In the secret place of His tabernacle*
> *He shall hide me;*
> *He shall set me high upon a rock."*
>
> Psalm 27:4–5

Having chosen the path God has ordained for us, we no longer belong to ourselves but have joined with Him in obedience to His revealed will. We are no longer our own, but everything we say, do and think should be about and for Him, as we cannot serve two masters. When we belong to Father God, it is a full-time, life commitment.

Overview

The parable of the Prodigal Son illustrates themes of rebellion, forgiveness, redemption, and the complexities of family relationships.

Characters

Younger Son

- Demands his inheritance from his father, symbolising rebellion.
- Wastes wealth on prodigal living in a distant country.
- Faces hardship and hunger, contemplates returning home.

Older Son

- Remains obedient but harbours resentment towards his brother.
- Condemns the younger son's actions upon his return.

Father

- Represents compassion, unconditional love and forgiveness.
- Saw son from afar and ran to embrace him, breaking social norms.

Cultural Context

- The parable occurs within a close-knit community.
- The Kezazah Ceremony shamed failed people who returned.
- The father's actions defy society's expectations and demonstrate grace.

Themes

- Rebellion and Consequences
- The younger son's demand signifies a wish for independence.
- His journey leads to suffering and self-realisation.
- Forgiveness and Grace
- The father's readiness to forgive highlights grace.
- The act of running to his son shows love surpassing society's expectations.
- Community and Shame.
- Cultural context of the Jewish community plays a role.
- The concept of "Kezazah" represents community rejection.

Judgment and Comparison

- The older brother's judgment contrasts with the father's love.
- Encourages reflection on personal attitudes towards forgiveness.

Reflections

- The younger son comes to his senses, realising his father's servants live better.
- He returns, not expecting to be treated as a son but as a servant.
- The father's embrace signifies acceptance and reconciliation despite social norms.

The Lost Son Redeemed

"But the father said to his servants,
'Bring out the best robe and put it on him,
and put a ring on his hand and sandals on his feet.
And bring the fatted calf here and kill it,
and let us eat and be merry;
for this my son was dead and is alive again;
he was lost and is found.'
And they began to be merry."

Luke 15:22–24

It is always the unexpected takes us by surprise. For this wayward son, his return had proven so different to what he expected. His father already embraced him, but there's more to follow. The father does four more things, to the amazement of all those who witnessed the return of his son. We are told:

"The father said to his servants,
'Bring out the best robe and put it on him,
and put a ring on his hand
and sandals on his feet.

And bring the fatted calf here and kill it,
and let us eat and be merry."

Luke 15:22–23

As the father walked with his son from outside the village, one could imagine all the villagers watched as the father ran past their homes to the road entering their village. Curiosity had taken over as they watched how the father embraced the one now recognised as his younger son.

The Prodigal son was so different to when he left, but this did not deter the father as he embraced his lost son and kissed him. As the villagers watched, some could have muttered to themselves, maybe hid the pottery jar in their hand in readiness. What the father did as he walked side by side with his son past them all was a testament to the village about unconditional love and grace.

As all the people stood together in the communal courtyard from which each of their homes led, gathered to hear what the father would say, were any expecting what was about to happen? To their amazement, the father gave orders to his servants to give his young son the best robe, a ring, and sandals.

What did each of the four items represent to the Prodigal and those witnessing what had happened?

a. The Best Robe. In having the best robe placed on him, the father was telling the Prodigal, as well as all observers, his position as son was restored. It was an immediate demonstration of complete approval, love, mercy, and protection.

In the book of Zechariah, he was told to remove from Joshua the high priest, his filthy garments and replace them with rich robes. Dressed in rich robes, Joshua stood clean and free (Zechariah 3:4–5). This spoke of the great favour Joshua found with God and the fact all condemnation of the law had been removed from him.

Dressed in the best robe, demonstrated the love the father had for his son. He now stands clean and free. Jesus also had a robe placed on him:

> *"And they put on Him a purple robe.*
> *Now the tunic was without seam,*
> *woven from the top in one piece."*
>
> John 19:2a, 23b

While this was prophecy, could His Father have been saying, "It's nearly over, Son. You are totally acceptable, clean in My sight?"

b. The Ring. Presenting a ring to someone was a sign of great affection and authority. Pharaoh removed his signet ring and put it on Joseph's hand (Genesis 41:42). King Ahasuerus took off his ring, the royal signet, and gave it to Mordecai (Esther 8:2). The ring proved Pharaoh's affection for Joseph and the King's affection for Mordecai which transferred to them all power and authority necessary for the promotions they received, one as Governor and the other as Prime Minister.

The ring placed on the hand of the Prodigal evidenced the great affection the father had toward him. The son received restoration of status, authority, and belonging within the family. The ring, along with the sandals, signified the son was no longer a servant or a slave, but was fully accepted back as a son with rights and privileges.

> *"God also demonstrates*
> *His own love toward us,*
> *in that while we were still sinners,*
> *Christ died for us."*
>
> Romans 5:8

c. *The Sandals.* As the Prodigal returned home without sandals, was a sign of being extremely destitute because in ancient biblical times, only servants and slaves went barefoot. Barefoot implied one was deprived of normal dress. It was also an indication of raw emotion, or mourning, if a person appeared barefoot in public. David exhibited this when he climbed the Mount of Olives. 2 Samuel 15:30

When the father ordered sandals to be brought out and put on his son's feet, he was silently saying for the third and final time, this restored child of mine was not to be treated as a servant but as a son with all entitlements. It was several years later, Jesus climbed the Mount of Olives and entered the Garden of Gethsemane (Luke 22:39). With raw emotion, He met with His Father on Holy Ground. Was He sandal-less?

d. *The Fatted Calf.* The verse reads:

> *"And bring the fatted calf here and kill it,*
> *and let us eat and be merry."*
>
> Luke 15:23

The word "kill" (Strong's 2380) means "to sacrifice". It was a customary practice when a public celebration was held in Israel, it began with a sacrifice, and the meat from it was used in the feast. The father gave the family blessing to his son, but it was in connection with the sacrifice of the fatted calf.

In the Old Testament, when a sacrifice was offered up, the fat was burned on the altar to the Lord. The fat of the sacrificial animal represented the richest and most excellent part of the animal. Job sacrificed daily in case his children had sinned. Job 1:5

The father did not just offer up a calf, but he offered up the fatted calf, his best. The father gave the Prodigal son his robe, ring, sandals, and his fatted calf as a sacrifice. They came as a complete package. To understand what the father did, we need to revisit what the son said to his father.

> *"Father, I have sinned*
> *against heaven and in your sight,*
> *and am no longer worthy*
> *to be called your son."*

Luke 15:21

As the text is reviewed, the words to focus on are *"against heaven and in your sight"*. What the younger son did was in the sight of his father, not anything supposedly occurred when he was away in another country. The younger son is referring to his demand to receive his share of the family inheritance, a situation between himself and his father before he left.

The question to be asked is, "What sin did the son commit?" The older brother imagined all types of sins, which he later related to his father. But this is a moment between the father and the younger son, where the wisdom of the father prevailed. The son had broken the fourth commandment:

> *"Honour your father and your mother,*
> *that your days may be long upon the land*
> *which the Lord your God is giving you."*

Exodus 20:12

To validate the son had not committed the sins the older brother later accused him of doing, we read the following verse about the younger son:

The Prodigal Son

> *"He would gladly have filled his stomach*
> *with the pods that the swine ate,*
> *and no one gave him anything."*
>
> Luke 15:16

When the younger son was on his own, out of sight, where no one knew what he was doing, he could have secretly taken some of the pigs' food for himself, but he didn't. Why would he have committed the other things the older brother accused him of openly, in front of those Gentiles he was living with?

The father understood his returned son required restoration with Father God, so he said to his servants:

> *"Bring out the best robe and put it on him."*
>
> Luke 15:22a

Another question has presented itself: "What was the best robe he told his son to wear?" The best robe would have been his father's own *"Prayer Shawl"* or his *"Tallit"*. The father knew the son required to have a time of prayer with Father God, in the secrecy of his own closet. The *"Prayer Shawl"* would provide such a place for the communion of his son with Father God. Matthew 6:6

As the son has a time of confession and renewal secretly with Father God, the son's father says:

"And bring the fatted calf here and kill it."

Luke 15:23a

The father ordered a sacrifice, a peace offering, not a sin offering, to be offered for his son. If the younger son had committed all the older brother accused him of, a sin offering would have been necessary. So what is the difference between a *"Sin Offering"* and a *"Peace Offering"*?

The primary difference between a *"Sin Offering"* and a *"Peace Offering"* lies in their purpose. A *"Sin Offering"* was a mandatory sacrifice for atonement of sins, while a *"Peace Offering"* was a voluntary offering expressing gratitude, fellowship, and joy with Father God.

Here's a more detailed breakdown:

Sin Offering:

- **Purpose:** To atone for unintentional sins or defilement.
- **Mandatory:** Required for specific transgressions or ritual impurity.
- **Focus:** Deals with the issue of sin itself and the need for forgiveness.
- **Ritual:** Specific procedures were prescribed for different types of sin.
- **Partaking:** In some cases, the offerer and priests could partake of the meat.

Peace Offering:

- **Purpose:** To express thanksgiving, fellowship, and joy with Father God.
- **Voluntary:** Offerers brought it freely, often as a result of blessings received.
- **Focus:** Celebrates the relationship and communion between Father God and the offerer.
- **Ritual:** Involves feasting on the sacrificed animal with family and friends, symbolising fellowship.
- **Partaking:** Offerers and their families, along with the priests, ate a portion of the animal.

In essence, the *"Sin Offering"* was a necessary step to address sin and restore a relationship with Father God, while the *"Peace Offering"* was a joyful expression of a restored relationship and fellowship between the father and his younger son.

The peace offering was written down by Moses as to what was to be carried out.

> *"When his offering is a sacrifice of a peace offering,*
> *if he offers it of the herd, whether male or female,*
> *he shall offer it without blemish before the Lord.*
>
> *And he shall lay his hand on the head of his offering,*
> *and kill it at the door of the tabernacle of meeting;*

and Aaron's sons, the priests,
shall sprinkle the blood all around on the altar.

Then he shall offer from the sacrifice of the peace offering
an offering made by fire to the Lord.

The fat that covers the entrails
and all the fat that is on the entrails,
the two kidneys and the fat that is on them by the flanks,
and the fatty lobe attached to the liver above the kidneys,
he shall remove;

and Aaron's sons shall burn it on the altar upon the burnt sacrifice,
which is on the wood that is on the fire,
as an offering made by fire, a sweet aroma to the Lord."

Leviticus 3:1–5

Forgiveness would be empty without restoration to the privileges forfeited by sin. Therefore, if you bear the name son or daughter through having received Jesus as Lord and Saviour by the power of the Holy Spirit, you have found favour with the Father.

The best robe has been placed upon you, a demonstration of the Father's complete approval of you and love and protection for you. A ring has been put on your hand representing the riches you have in Christ, the authority you're given in the name of Jesus and installation into the office of king and priest to Father God. Sandals have been put on your feet, affirming sonship and all of its benefits, including but not limited to healing, lovingkindness, tender mercies and every good thing.

As the father set the tone for the whole village through forgiveness and grace, the son communed with Father God, the fatted calf slaughtered, and the appropriate parts offered as a *"Peace Offering"* to Father God. As this was done, the festivities began with singing and dancing. Maybe it would be a good time to read Psalm 103.

> *"Bless the Lord, O my soul;*
> *and all that is within me,*
> *bless His holy name!*
>
> *Bless the Lord, O my soul,*
> *and forget not all His benefits:*
> *who forgives all your iniquities,*
> *who heals all your diseases,*
> *who redeems your life from destruction,*
> *who crowns you with*
> *lovingkindness and tender mercies."*
>
> Psalm 103:1–4

Father God provides for us, allowing us to choose our life's path. God's love compels Him to give us "free will" to either obey or reject Him. Though we reject Him, Father God never rejects us. He lovingly awaits our coming to Him, longing to receive and restore us, without hesitation. He offers us a Robe. Forgiveness, covering our sin and shame (love, grace). A Ring. Restored identity and belonging to His family (value). Sandals. Renewed purpose and meaning for life (hope).

The Fatted Calf is offering the very best to Father God. His Son Jesus, who became the sacrificial lamb, the perfect sacrifice for our sins, was the very best sacrifice, as no one else was acceptable.

Overview

The story of the Prodigal Son illustrates themes of love, forgiveness, and restoration through the father's actions.

The Father's Gifts

The Best Robe:
- Represents the son's restored position and the father's love.
- Symbolises approval and protection.

The Ring:
- Signifies affection, authority and belonging.
- Restores the son's status within the family.

The Sandals:
- Indicates the son's transition from servant to son.
- Symbolises entitlement and belonging.

The Fatted Calf:
- Exemplifies the best offering to Father God, relating to the joy of Redemption.
- Represents a significant sacrifice and a celebration, symbolising the joy of the son's return.
- Denotes gratitude and joy in the restored relationship.

Sin Offering vs. Peace Offering

Sin Offering:
- Mandatory for atonement of sins.
- Focuses on forgiveness.

Peace Offering:
- Voluntary, expressing thanksgiving and joy.
- Celebrates the relationship with Father God.

Themes of Forgiveness

- Emphasises that Forgiveness must come with Restoration.
- The father's actions showcase his willingness to embrace and welcome the son back without hesitation.
- Father God offers similar Grace and Restoration to all who return to Him.

The Self-Righteous Elder Brother

Now his older son was in the field.
And as he came and drew near to the house,
he heard music and dancing.
So he called one of the servants
and asked what these things meant.

And he said to him, "Your brother has come,
and because he has received him safe and sound,
your father has killed the fatted calf."
But he was angry and would not go in.

Therefore his father came out and pleaded with him.
So he answered and said to his father,
"Lo, these many years I have been serving you;
I never transgressed your commandment at any time;
and yet you never gave me a young goat,
that I might make merry with my friends.
But as soon as this son of yours came,

> *who has devoured your livelihood with harlots,*
> *you killed the fatted calf for him."*
>
> *And he said to him, "Son, you are always with me,*
> *and all that I have is yours.*
> *It was right that we should make merry and be glad,*
> *for your brother was dead and is alive again,*
> *and was lost and is found."*

Luke 15:25–32

Jesus continued His teaching with the older brother taking centre stage. Was anyone expecting what Jesus was sharing? Were James and Matthew aware Jesus was not only teaching all those gathered, but suggesting the animosity between the two be put aside, as reconciliation between them both was not an option?

While the older brother was out working, overseeing the workers, much had transpired in the village, and he was unaware. Returning home, he inquired about the music and dancing, and was not impressed because he wasn't told the younger brother returned, and his father organised a feast to celebrate.

I did notice the father omitted to alert the older son to the return home and his reconciliation with the younger son. Perhaps the father was hesitant to inform his older son, his brother returned home, because he observed the previous relationship between the two brothers and was more understanding about the younger son's position. In trying to protect the younger son, the father anticipated the older son would be angry and vengeful.

This could almost be a parallel situation to Cain and Abel. Cain instigated a sacrifice between them both to the Lord, but when Cain was rejected, he became angry. Here we have the father who accepted the younger son back, and the older brother is angry. Genesis 4:8

We need to take a few steps back to understand what hadn't happened in the past and should have transpired for a clear picture of what is taking place. On the one hand, we have the sin of the law-breaker, and on the other, the sin of the law-keeper, as both centre on broken relationships. One breaks the expectations of family and society, while the other breaks his relationship with the father, while he fulfilled the same expectations.

The older son would have been present or have been told about the altercation between his father and his younger brother when the brother first wanted to leave. In their culture, the older brother's responsibility was to bring reconciliation between the two as mediator, but he did and said nothing. The village was expecting a mediation to occur, and expecting a different outcome.

The older brother's silent refusal to be involved could be the root cause of the younger brother's leaving. The arrogance of the older brother may have contributed to the break between father and younger son. When the time came for the brother to leave, the older brother should have pleaded with the son to remain for the sake of the father, but if he was defiant and left, then prayer offered for his safe travel and well-being, but again, silence ruled.

The older brother's refusal indicated a broken relationship with his father, as the situation is not as it should be between himself, his younger brother and the father. So, what were the words Jesus used when telling this parable?

"So he divided to them his livelihood."

Luke15:12b

Both sons received their share of the family land, but not the right of authority, which remained with the father. While the younger son chose to dispose of his share, the father did not stop him, although the older son gained the right of possession, he did not dispose of what he received.

When the father was aware the older son refused to join the festivities:

The father came out and pleaded with him.
So he answered and said to his father,
"Lo, these many years I have been serving you;
I never transgressed your commandment at any time;
and yet you never gave me a young goat,
that I might make merry with my friends.
But as soon as this son of yours came,

> *who has devoured your livelihood with harlots,*
> *you killed the fatted calf for him."*

Luke 15:28b–30

When the older son approached the home, as he heard music, the natural reaction would be the pleasure of a delightful evening. Once inside the home, his father would share with him the reason for the occasion. But the son did not do this, as he inquired about what was taking place from one of the servants. The servant replied:

> *"Your brother has come ,*
> *and because he has received him*
> *safe and sound,*
> *your father has killed the fatted calf."*

Luke 15:27

When the older brother heard the word *"safe and sound"* or "hygiaino", which translated meant "good health", he should have rushed at once to the banquet because such a report meant the father hadn't decided what to do with the prodigal. The older son would naturally want to ensure justice was carried out, but as the word also meant "shalom" or "peace", the father had already received the prodigal "with peace", then the two were reconciled.

The banquet was organised, not for the prodigal, but so the father could celebrate with his friends about the reconciliation taken place between himself and the younger son. At the banquet, the father would sit with the guests, as the older brother would act as an overseer of all the festivities.

What the father was saying, because the invited guests were celebrating in his home, the older son would serve as a servant to them, serving all who had gathered. The problem is, the younger brother is one of the invited guests, and the older brother is expected to serve him along with the other guests his father had invited. Could he bring himself to serve, wait on the younger brother whom he despised?

The older son could quite easily justify his actions as he believed the father dishonoured the family in the eyes of the village and the community. Reconciliation and Restoration without penalty paid for by the offender is too much for the older brother to understand or accept. For him, grace is not only amazing, it is also infuriating.

The duty of the older son in their culture meant he would greet each guest as they arrived, even if he could not stay for the proceedings. Failure to fulfil this courtesy was a personal insult to the guests and to the father as host. The older son is very aware of his obligations; therefore, his action is an intentional public insult to the father.

When the father is told the older son refused to join the celebration, the guests are well aware of the situation, as nothing is secret in the village, which highlighted the rebellious nature of the older son towards the father. The older son had committed a very serious sin, as all the guests would expect retribution of the older son would follow.

For the second time on the same day, the father's response is not what everyone was expecting. Again, he endures shame and a self-emptying love to reconcile.

As the older son refused to participate in the celebration, the father went out into the courtyard, where the older son verbally accused both his father and brother in public. In doing so, he insulted his father in front of all the guests. The older son has successfully severed his relationship with his father.

So, what had the father subjected himself to once again, and what was the responsibility of the older son? As the older son remained silent, he refused to fulfil the sacred responsibility the village custom had placed on him. For his own reasons, he doesn't want reconciliation but justice. Even if he hated his brother, he should have fulfilled the task for his father.

As we look at the older son and examine his thoughts and actions, although he saw himself as righteous, we can note the following:

- Refused to participate in reconciliation.
- Rebelled against the father.
- Broke a relationship, not the law.
- Accused the father of favouritism.

- Removed himself from his family.
- Refused partnership with his father.
- Despised his brother.
- Spoke unfounded lies about his brother.
- He saw himself as a servant, not a son.
- He required forgiveness from his father and brother.
- He was consumed with envy, pride, bitterness, sarcasm, anger, resentment, self-centeredness, hate, self-satisfaction, and self-deception.

The older brother condemned the younger brother and his actions while he was away, but how did he know or presume what his little brother was up to? This says a lot about what was happening before the younger son left. The younger son might have been a rebellious child, but he was given teachings in his childhood he adhered to, similar to Joseph, Moses and David.

The older son emphasised the law, and the law said the father's younger son was to be excommunicated from the village and their family. Here, we can see the older son is similar to the scribes and the Pharisees, who were the supposed keepers of the law. Does James the Zealot fit into this category? Matthew, the customs officer, certainly fits the younger brother whom Jesus redeemed and told to follow Him.

The actions and words of the older son revealed his attitude and motive toward his father, as everything he did for his father was based on works and merit. He had now broken the same commandment as his younger brother, as he justified himself. He said to his father:

> *"Lo, these many years*
> *I have been serving you;*
> *I never transgressed your commandment*
> *at any time."*

Luke 15:29

In saying these words, he pointed out to the father he had been obedient, slaving away for years, but never received credit or rewards for his work. He despised the father's response to the younger brother, as he had no understanding of Grace. He disowned his younger brother, referring to him as *"this son of yours"*. The true feeling of the older brother had surfaced, as he thought their father was mean and uncaring, but this was far from the truth. Who is the Prodigal son now?

The older son never arrived at the realisation everything he desired was waiting for him to claim, but he did not understand. The wise father knew how to deal with the grievance in the heart of the wayward older son when he said:

> *"Son, you are always with me,*
> *and all that I have is yours."*

Luke 15:31

The older brother's focus was on himself and his service; as a result, he had no joy in his brother's arrival home. He was so consumed with justice, he failed to see the value of his brother's repentance and return. The older brother had allowed bitterness to take root in his heart to the point he was unable to show compassion toward his brother.

The father was a wise man and knew how to deal with every situation. He could have been angry, exploded, criticised his elder son in the same way as he had spoken to his father, but he didn't. The older son had dishonoured his father in front of everyone, so what separated him from the earlier dealings of the younger brother?

The father applies divine wisdom to this situation with the words:

> *"Son, you are always with me,*
> *and all that I have is yours.*
> *It was right that we should make merry and be glad,*
> *for your brother was dead and is alive again,*
> *and was lost and is found."*
>
> Luke 15:31–32

The word *"son"* should be noted as used by the father. There are two words used in this passage. Firstly, the older son used "huios", which meant to distinguish a descendant representing the family, but the father chose "tekon", which denotes the natural relationship of a child to their parents. Very gently, the father corrected only one point in what the older brother said and reminded him, the prodigal is *"your brother"*.

The bitterness spilled over into the elder brother's relationships, as he was unable to forgive the perceived sin of his father against him. Rather than enjoy fellowship with his father, brother, and community, the older brother stayed outside the house and nursed his anger. How sad to choose misery and isolation over restoration and reconciliation.

The parable has no ending, as we don't know what the older son eventually decided. Will the older son enter the banquet and start acting like his father, or will he refuse to accept his father's offer of costly, unearned love? I could imagine the words of Moses to the children of Israel are applicable when he said:

> *"I call heaven and earth*
>
> *as witnesses today against you,*
>
> *that I have set before you life and death,*
>
> *blessing and cursing;*
>
> *therefore choose life,*
>
> *that both you*
>
> *and your descendants may live."*

Deuteronomy 30:19

Overview

The parable of the Prodigal Son illustrates the contrasting responses of the two brothers, particularly the older brother's anger and self-righteousness.

The Older Brother's Anger

- The older brother returned from the field and heard music.
- He learned his younger brother returned and was angry about the celebration.
- He confronted his father, highlighting his years of service and lack of reward.
- He referred to the younger brother as *"this son of yours,"* showing disdain.

Themes of Self-Righteousness

- The older brother's actions mirror the attitudes of the Pharisees.
- He believed he deserved recognition for his obedience to the law.
- His bitterness prevented him from celebrating his brother's return and repentance.

The Father's Response

- The father gently pleads with the older son, affirming everything he has belonged to him.
- He emphasised the importance of celebrating the younger brother's return as a matter of life and death.

Deeper Analysis

- The older brother's unwillingness to reconcile exposed his own broken relationship with the father, despite outward obedience.
- He failed his cultural role as mediator and allowed bitterness, pride, and legalism to take root.
- The father's response is consistently gracious and loving, even as he is publicly shamed by both sons.
- The story ends unresolved, questioning whether the older brother will choose reconciliation or remain in self-imposed isolation.

Lack of Resolution

- The parable raises questions about Acceptance, Grace, and Reconciliation.

THE UNJUST STEWARD

"For the sons of this world are more shrewd
in their generation than the sons of light.
And I say to you,
make friends for yourselves by unrighteous mammon,
that when you fail,
they may receive you into an everlasting home."

Luke 16:8b–9

"No servant can serve two masters;
for either he will hate the one and love the other,
or else he will be loyal to the one
and despise the other.
You cannot serve God and mammon."

Luke 16:13

Jesus left Capernaum and was in the last part of His ministry in the Judean and Perean areas, and it was Winter. Within a couple of weeks, Jesus would make His way to Bethany, where He raised Lazarus from the dead. Not long after this, Jesus will complete His final journey to Jerusalem in the Spring.

Jesus turned His attention to His disciples. You would remember, only some weeks before, Jesus had sent out seventy to minister (Luke 10:1). We need to understand, Jesus had many followers, and some were disciples; also, women were part of His group. Add to this number the tax collectors and sinners, along with the Pharisees and scribes (Luke 15:1–2a), many gathered to hear the teaching of Jesus.

Jesus addressed the core teaching of the last three parables, the "Lost Sheep", the "Lost Coin", and the "Prodigal Son" in the parable of the "Unjust Steward". This parable is usually overlooked as not being a part of the big three. So, how does this parable fit in?

Previously, we noticed the conflict between two disciples, James and Matthew. The scribes and Pharisees were also antagonistic to Jesus and His followers, not only the disciples. In the previous parables, the "Lost Sheep", the "Lost Coin" and the "Prodigal Son", the one who was hurting the most in each case was the shepherd, the woman and the father, not the sheep, the coin or the son. So how does this parable of the "Unjust Steward" Jesus shared relate to the three previous parables?

In this story, we have a rich man and an unjust steward, an employee. The employee was responsible for managing the business for the rich man. Things had gotten out of hand, and an accusation was made to the rich man about the unjust steward.

The unjust steward, thinking he was about to lose his job, decided to gain favour with the customers by reducing their debt. When the rich man found out what he had done, he praised the manager for his actions, as some repayment was better than nothing.

The thing to note is, the unjust steward went and did exactly what he had been accused of doing. I guess a situation can't get any worse than what you have been accused of, so why not use whatever has been said to your advantage? This is certainly worldly thinking.

But Jesus said:

> *"For the sons of this world are more shrewd*
> *in their generation than the sons of light."*
>
> Luke 16:8b

Jesus was not giving praise for the actions of the unjust steward, but drawing a picture of the world compared to eternal issues. The rich man and the unjust steward were only concerned about the here and now, where Jesus was intimating, more was at stake.

Jesus' last words of this parable say:

> *"No servant can serve two masters;*
> *for either he will hate the one and love the other,*
> *or else he will be loyal to the one*

and despise the other.
You cannot serve God and mammon."

Luke 16:13

These words were heard by the Pharisees, who took offence at what Jesus said, because they were lovers of money (v14), but this wasn't about money only, but about "Means" and "Relationships".

As we reread the passage of scripture, there are two groups mentioned: those of the world and those who belong to the *"Light"*. You would remember, Jesus previously said in Jerusalem, not long after the *Feast of Tabernacles*:

"I am the light of the world.
He who follows Me
shall not walk in darkness,
but have the light of life."

John 8:12

Jesus went on to share how those of the world live and deceive each other to survive, as one took advantage of the other. Jesus is saying, worldly people expect to be treated favourably by those they have favoured. This is the story of the rich man and the unjust steward. A story of fraud and mistrust on the part of both of them. Jesus was teaching, the people of the *"Light"* could expect those not of the *"Light"*, the world, to take advantage of them whenever they could.

Jesus continued with His teaching. If those in the world saw this as a way to survive in this life, surely those of the *"Light"* should mimic the people of the world, but with a purer motive, pertaining to eternal life. If the worldly people saw it necessary to make plans for their immediate future, shouldn't the people of the *"Light"* be making plans for their eternal future?

Only a few weeks would pass until Jesus gave further teaching about this very subject when He taught:

> *"Lay up for yourselves treasure in heaven,*
> *where neither moth nor rust destroys*
> *and where thieves do not break in and steal.*
> *For where your treasure is,*
> *there your heart will be also."*

Matthew 6:20-21

Jesus was teaching His followers to use their God given "Means" to glorify Father God. This is so much more than money. You would bring to mind the words Jesus spoke to those who would inherit *"Eternal Life"*:

*"Come, you blessed of My Father,
inherit the kingdom prepared for you
from the foundation of the world:*

*for I was hungry and you gave Me food;
I was thirsty and you gave Me drink;
I was a stranger and you took me in;
I was naked and you clothed Me;
I was sick and you visited Me;
I was in prison and you came to Me.*

*Inasmuch as you did it to one
of the least of these My brethren,
you did it to Me."*

Matthew 25:34–36, v40

The people of the *"Called"* used their God given "Means" to glorify Father God. These people were aware of Jesus' kingdom promise when He said:

*"For what profit is it to a man
if he gains the whole world,
and loses his own soul?*

> *Or what will a man give*
> *in exchange for his soul?"*
>
> Matthew 16:26

While the Pharisees and those of the world were lovers of money, those who are in the *"Light"* know it is not about money but all about "Means". The worldly concentrate on the here and now, but the *"children of light"* focus on the future. They knew and were assured all their needs would be supplied, because Jesus had taught:

> *"Therefore I tell you, do not worry about your life,*
> *what you will eat; or about your body,*
> *what you will wear.*
> *For life is more than food,*
> *and the body more than clothes.*
>
> *Consider the ravens:*
> *They do not sow or reap,*
> *they have no storeroom or barn;*
> *yet God feeds them.*
> *And how much more valuable you are than birds!*

Redeemed

Who of you by worrying can add a single hour to your life?
Since you cannot do this very little thing,
why do you worry about the rest?

Consider how the wild flowers grow.
They do not labour or spin.
Yet I tell you, not even Solomon
in all his splendour was dressed like one of these.

If that is how God clothes the grass of the field,
which is here today,
and tomorrow is thrown into the fire,
how much more will He clothe you,
you of little faith!

And do not set your heart
on what you will eat or drink;
do not worry about it.
For the pagan world runs after all such things,
and your Father knows that you need them.

The Unjust Steward

> *But seek His kingdom,*
> *and these things will be given to you as well."*
>
> Luke 12:22–31 (NIV)

Paul, many years later, would reassure the Philippians when he wrote to them:

> *"Father God shall supply all your need*
> *according to His riches in glory by Christ Jesus."*
>
> Philippians 4:19

Just as the followers of Jesus were warned and taught what to expect from those who are not like-minded to themselves, so we can expect the same, as human nature does not change except for the grace of Father God. While the rich appear to become richer, the well-to-dos always have the best, and many of us struggle, we need to stay focused because we have all our needs met, not our wants.

Part of Jesus' final teaching touches on this very subject. What can we expect as followers of Jesus, as we are part of Him who is the *"Light"*?

> *"If you were of the world,*
> *the world would love its own.*
> *Yet because you are not of the world,*

but I chose you out of the world,
therefore the world hates you."

John 15:19

We, just like the disciples and followers, rely on the Holy Spirit to guide us in all things. We should never be discouraged, as we remember to take everything to Father God in prayer, knowing He hears and answers as He desires us to grow in Him.

Jesus was saying to His disciples, they were lost sheep who had been found; some had lost their identity and were considered outcasts by their own. Because the Father loved each one and called them to Himself, they had been restored to their rightful place and been clothed in garments as they are now family, children who belong to the Father.

While many still lost choose to focus on the world and what it offered, the disciples were to remain in the love which redeemed and called them to fulfil a greater role. For the disciples, there was no compromise, as they were to keep their eyes centred on Father God, the *"Light"*, not the world.

The disciples were not to seek the praise of men but to always complete the task set before them, no matter what the cost. This way, they would be praising Father God and not themselves, although the road ahead would be fraught with challenges, and in their own strength would fail.

Those who followed the leading of the Holy Spirit were to remember, you can't serve two masters, and to never forget what the future held for those of the *"Called"*. By remaining in His love, their eternal destiny would be secure.

Overview

The text discusses the parable of the Unjust Steward and its implications for followers of Jesus regarding the use of resources and eternal values.

Context

- Jesus is nearing the end of His ministry.
- He addressed His disciples and a large crowd, including sinners and Pharisees.

The Parable

- The parable involved a rich man and an unjust steward.
- The unjust steward reduced debts to gain favour before losing his job.
- Jesus highlighted the shrewdness of worldly people versus the expectations for those in the *"Light"*.

Key Teachings

<u>Serving Two Masters</u>:
- You cannot serve both Father God and money.
- Pharisees, who love money, are offended by His teaching.

<u>Earthly vs. Eternal Focus</u>:
- Worldly people focus on immediate gains.
- Followers of Jesus should plan for eternal rewards using their resources wisely.

<u>Jesus as the Light</u>:
- Those who follow Jesus should reflect His values and not succumb to worldly ways.
- True needs will be met by Father God, not just wants.

Conclusion of Teachings

- Jesus reassured followers, Father God will supply their needs.
- Followers can expect to be challenged by the world, but should remain faithful.
- Expect opposition from those focused on earthly things, but remain centred on Father God.
- Followers are called to stay faithful and focused on their eternal relationship with Father God.

THE LAW, THE PROPHETS, AND THE KINGDOM

"You are those
who justify yourselves before men,
but God knows your hearts.
For what is highly esteemed among men
is an abomination in the sight of God."

Luke 16:15

From teaching the crowd comprising His disciples, women followers, tax collectors, sinners, scribes and Pharisees, Jesus focused His attention and remarks from His disciples to the Pharisees who ridiculed Jesus for His teaching, as what He taught contradicted their beliefs.

Jesus told the Pharisees bluntly, their problem was they justified themselves, not Father God. This was nothing new, as at least one Old Testament Prophet did the same.

> *"Though He slay me,*
> *yet will I trust Him.*
> *Even so,*
> *I will defend my own ways before Him."*
>
> Job 13:15

Although Job was protected, rich and prosperous, he had one fault Father God chose to correct. *Job justified himself rather than being justified by God.*

Father God instigated the conversation with Satan and used him to accomplish a predetermined work in the life of Job. Satan fell into Father God's trap and was unaware. So, what was Father God's hidden agenda? Let me share the following verse with you.

> *"Elihu, the son of Barachel the Buzite,*
> *of the family of Ram was aroused against Job;*
> *his wrath was aroused,*
> *because Job justified himself rather than God."*
>
> Job 32:2

When Job was shown the error of his ways, he sincerely sought forgiveness, which was obtained, and he was right with Father God, for Job confessed:

> *"I know that You can do everything,*
> *and that no purpose of Yours*
> *can be withheld from You."*

Job 42:2

Unlike Job, the Pharisees refused to repent because they were lovers of money (Luke 16:14a). Jesus, in His remarks to them, included His Father's words to the prophet Samuel when He said:

> *"Do not look at his appearance*
> *or at his physical stature,*
> *because I have refused him.*
> *For the Lord does not see as man sees;*
> *for man looks at the outward appearance,*
> *but the Lord looks at the heart."*

1 Samuel 16:7

Appearance was of the utmost priority to most of the Pharisees. Some were warm to the teaching of Jesus, like Nicodemus, but not these Pharisees. Most were involved in fraud within the temple worship, as the money changers would extort those who came to worship; those who sold the animals for sacrifices would fabricate excuses to reject their unblemished animals, finding fault with the animals to be sacrificed and selling another animal to take its place, while recycling the confiscated one.

Jesus had already exposed their ruthless dealings when He cleansed the temple the first time, as He said:

> *"Take these things away!*
> *Do not make My Father's house*
> *a house of merchandise!"*

John 2:16

Little did the Pharisees realise Jesus would cleanse the temple a second time, which would certainly damage their expectations of more wealth.

> *"My house shall be called a house of prayer,*
> *but you have made it a den of thieves."*

Matthew 21:13

The religious leaders were focused on outward appearance rather than inner transformation. Jesus condemned their hypocrisy, pointing out they were trying to justify themselves before men, while Father God saw their hearts.

Jesus had emphasised faithfulness, as Father God tested the Pharisees' ability to handle spiritual riches, rather than worldly wealth. Jesus implied, all they had belonged to His Father, and the resources given to them were the crucial point. How the Pharisees managed their resources was of more importance than their outward appearance.

Jesus had left them in no doubt when He said:

> *"No servant can serve two masters;*
> *for either he will hate the one and love the other,*
> *or else he will be loyal to one and despise the other.*
> *You cannot serve God and mammon."*
>
> Luke 16:13

What these Pharisees did not understand was true greatness lay in faithfulness, humility and devotion to Father God, not in worldly wealth and appearance. They did not understand true devotion to Father God required prioritising spiritual values over material possessions.

As the Pharisees were *"lovers of money"*, they looked upon wealth as a sign of Father God's blessing and poverty as a sign of His judgment. Jesus continued to address this issue, teaching material possessions are a trust from Father God to be used responsibly for good. One's attitude toward possessions was a clear indication of whether a person was living self-centeredly or under the total Lordship of Father God.

As Jesus continued with the parable of the "Rich Man and Lazarus", He challenged those with a godless view of wealth and righteousness to repent and help others with their resources. Jesus left them in no doubt, as what He was about to share was an example of *"what is highly esteemed among men, is an abomination in the sight of Father God."* Luke 16:15b

As Jesus told the parable about the Rich Man and Lazarus, found in Luke 16:19–31, the rich man had ignored the poor beggar who sat by his gate, and now they are both in the afterlife. The following observations are made. Things we note about the rich man are:

- He could see.
- He could talk.
- He could hear.
- He could touch.
- He could taste.
- He could reason.
- He was tormented.
- He had memory.

What we are told about Lazarus is, he had an advocate, who told the rich man:

> *"He is comforted*
> *and you are tormented."*
>
> Luke 16:25b

While the rich man had all his senses, Lazarus knew no pain or suffering, and possibly retained no remembrance of what he endured in his previous life. The fact the rich man could reason leads us to explore his request to father Abraham when he said:

> *"Father Abraham, have mercy on me,*
> *and send Lazarus that he may dip the tip of his finger*
> *in water and cool my tongue;*
> *for I am tormented in this flame."*
>
> Luke 16:24

Reading this verse, one could imagine the rich man just wanted some temporary relief from his present situation, but as with most requests from a man such as this, could he have another motive? What was the rich man's real intention in his request, which appeared to be a simple deed by Lazarus?

The question to be asked is, "Where would Lazarus obtain a single drop of water?" Because the story Jesus is telling is set in the afterlife, the only place where a drop of water could be obtained would be from the *"River of Life"*. But a further question is raised: "Why would this make a difference to the rich man?" I share with you the following verse of scripture:

> *"Death and life are in the power of the tongue,*
> *and those who love it will eat its fruit."*
>
> Proverbs 18:21

What the rich man asked Abraham was to send Lazarus to dip the tip of his finger in the *"River of Life"* and place that drop of water on his tongue, which would give the rich man life, not what he had, spiritual death. Abraham then explained this was impossible, as there was a great gulf between him and them.

One word is foremost when reading this story, and that is "Shrewdness". How often has this principle reoccurred throughout all the parables Jesus shared with His mixed audience? The word "Shrewdness" is defined: the quality of having or showing good powers of judgement. Showing quick, practical, cleverness. The Bible definition means: astute, sharp, clever, discerning, rigorous in practical matters.

In the parable of the "Lost Sheep", the shepherd was discerning as well as other things. He understood the sheep would not make its way home; it would just keep wandering, then lie down and become *"cast down"*, open to any predator.

In the parable of the "Lost Coin", the woman was clever, discerning, and diligent in practical matters. She understood the coin would not find itself, and rigorous work in sweeping the floor, aided by the light, was necessary for the coin to be found.

In the parable of the "Prodigal Son", the father was discerning, showing good powers of judgment. The younger son was astute, sharp and clever when he realised the only way home was through his father. The older son was not shrewd, as he possessed none of the qualities mentioned, but thought only about himself.

In the parable of the "Unjust Steward", the Rich Man and the Unjust Steward represented the Pharisees and the older son, who were of the world, but the children of *"Light"*, possessed the qualities of being astute, sharp, clever, discerning, rigorous in practical matters, showing good powers of judgement.

As Jesus shared the parable of the "Rich Man and Lazarus", all previously mentioned was nailing, one nail at a time, the lid on the coffin of the Pharisees and how they perceived their god, not Father God, the One Jesus taught and shared. Antagonism between the religious leaders and those who followed Jesus was the result.

Although the crowd heard what Jesus said, especially foretelling about His own suffering, death and resurrection (Luke 16:31), they had knowledge but no understanding. Had two disciples, James and Matthew, understood the teaching of Jesus? Did they become reconciled with each other? One would imagine they did, as both went on to share the teaching of Jesus, once the Holy Spirit was revealed at Pentecost. John 14:26

In one way, the rich man of Jesus' story was very different from the religious leaders, the Pharisees. He lived a life of gourmet excess and indulgence, but the Pharisees were rigid, disciplined and self-controlled. Yet they shared this with the rich man: they cared nothing for the needy around them, and despised them with neglect. That's why they were so offended when Jesus taught and cared for tax collectors and sinners. Luke 15:1–2

Overview

The text discusses Jesus' teachings on self-justification and the dangers of materialism, contrasting the attitudes of the Pharisees with true faithfulness to Father God.

Jesus' Teachings

- Jesus addressed the Pharisees, who ridiculed Him for His teachings.
- He emphasised Father God looks into the heart, not outward appearance.
- The Pharisees justified themselves instead of relying on Father God.

The Example of Job

- Job justified himself before Father God but ultimately sought forgiveness.
- Unlike Job, the Pharisees resisted correction and held onto their wealth.

Focus on Inner Transformation

- Pharisees prioritised outward appearance and wealth.
- Jesus highlighted true greatness through faithfulness and humility.
- Material possessions are a trust from Father God to be used responsibly.

The Parable of the Rich Man and Lazarus

- The Rich Man could see and reason, but was tormented after death.
- Lazarus found comfort in the afterlife despite his suffering on earth.
- The Rich Man's request for relief illustrated his lack of understanding.

The Concept of Shrewdness

- Shrewdness is highlighted through parables, showing good judgment and practical cleverness.
- Different characters in parables display varying degrees of discernment.

Conclusion on the Pharisees

- The teachings served to confront the Pharisees' perceptions of Father God and righteousness.
- Both the Rich Man and the Pharisees neglected the needy, which offended Jesus.

Conclusion:
LOST THINGS

Jesus shared great insights into the false thinking and the behaviour of the religious leaders, leading those who listened astray with their teaching and biases. Jesus, through His teaching, focused on the attitudes of the scribes and the Pharisees.

Their greatest downfall was the Pharisees chose riches as their god and did not attend to the well-being of those in their care. Jesus taught, money and the love of it should be your servant, not your god, dictating how you should act. Acquiring money is not wrong, but we are to use it to serve others in the Kingdom, under the promptings of the Holy Spirit.

While we often focus on ourselves, we need to remember how our riches affect Father God. The teaching Jesus brought was, those who became lost were to be found, rescued and brought back into the fold. While possessions were precious, losing even part of our inheritance could be devastating.

Through the actions of the Prodigal son:

- The father had a wounded heart.
- The father was always concerned for the son's welfare.

- The father waited patiently.
- The father was saying, "I'm not giving up on you."
- The father wanted him to return.

Sin destroys and deprives you of everything. We don't know when anyone will return, but when they do, they are to be welcomed home. The father didn't criticise the son by saying, "I told you so!" Father God welcomes us back when we get right with Him, as sin destroys character and self-esteem. As the father forgave and restored his son to his household, so should we with those who return.

Four things remain:

- Forgiveness.
- Acceptance.
- Restoration.
- Rejoicing.

Jesus taught His disciples, forgiveness and acceptance were to be given multiple times when the repentant sinner sought with true sincerity, resulting in restoration and rejoicing, for He said:

> *"Take heed to yourselves.*
> *If your brother sins against you,*
> *rebuke him;*

> *and if he repents, forgive him.*
> *And if he sins against you seven times in a day,*
> *and seven times in a day returns to you,*
> *saying, 'I repent,'*
> *you shall forgive him."*
>
> Luke 17:3–4

Redemption

Jesus taught the disciples, the crowds, and the Pharisees. Today, the Holy Spirit calls and talks to people. We each share the journey Jesus taught as we are all lost sheep. He seeks us out and calls us to Himself. When we have moved away from loving and serving Father God, like the Prodigal son, the Holy Spirit prompts us to return, and we find again the pearl of greatest price which we thought was lost. Matthew 13:45–46

If we stray and return to the fold, not everyone will be welcoming as we would hope, but the price has been paid by Jesus, and we are restored, maybe to another fellowship where Father God chooses us to be.

Not everyone goes astray, but some travel another path, as Father God blesses their work, but they worship their works, not Father God, although they believe what they are doing is acceptable, much like the Pharisees Jesus taught.

As followers of Jesus, we are to honour Father God first, not allowing anything to take His place. We can't serve Father God and man. Our true trust and loyalty belong only to Father God, who redeemed us and called us to Himself.

To stay close to Father God, walking and talking with Him daily is the first basic step, followed by obedience to His known will keeps our focus on Him. As sheep, we need to follow the Shepherd, be thankful for all He provides, confessing failures with true repentance to keep us close to Him in fellowship.

Several years ago, I heard the statement, "Get dressed before you get dressed," referring to the fact, you needed, as soon as you awake from sleep, to put on the "Armour of God", so you would be ready to face the battles of the day.

As the Holy Spirit brought fresh understanding with wisdom already given, He revealed a hidden detail I need to share with you. You still need to get dressed before you get dressed, but in a different manner.

Luke recorded the first time Jesus read the scripture in the Synagogue, when He was handed a scroll to read Isaiah 61. The thing is, Jesus stopped short, only reading the first part of verse two.

> *"The Spirit of the Lord God is upon Me,*
> *because the Lord has anointed Me*
> *to preach good tidings to the poor;*

> *He has sent Me to heal the broken hearted,*
> *to proclaim liberty to the captives,*
> *and the opening of the prison*
> *to those who are bound;*
> *to proclaim the acceptable year of the Lord."*

Isaiah 61:1–2a

It is not until you get partway through verse 3, the *"Garment of Praise"* is mentioned, as this part of the reading was reserved for a future time.

> *"To comfort all who mourn,*
> *to console those who mourn in Zion,*
> *to give them beauty for ashes,*
> *the oil of joy for mourning,*
> *the garment of praise for the*
> *spirit of heaviness."*

Isaiah 61:3

As I reread Paul's words about the *"Armour of God"* (Ephesians 6:10–17), there appeared to be no place for this *"Garment of Praise"* until I read the following verse.

> *"Praying always with all prayer*
> *and supplication in the Spirit,*

being watchful to this end with all perseverance

and supplication for all the saints."

Ephesians 6:18

I ask the question, "How does this work together?"

I need to retrace my steps and go back to the writings of Isaiah to understand what the people of his day understood about his reference to the *"Garment of Praise"* for this to work. Two garments of reference were worn. One was called a "Tallit", which was a prayer shawl worn over the shoulders, with tassels attached. This was used to make a tent where a person could meet with Father God in private, anywhere.

A second garment is called a "Tallit Katan", an undergarment in white used by the Jews, like a long singlet, put on first, and made of cotton or linen. The Jews use this garment in remembrance of the covenants made with Father God. Jesus mentioned this undergarment when He referred to the way the Pharisees dressed when He said:

"There was a certain rich man
who was clothed in purple
and fine linen and fared
sumptuously every day."

Luke 16:19

So, now I have the link. The "Tallit Katan" represents the *"Garment of Praise"* and the "Tallit" represents the *"Armour of God"*. A Jewish boy reaching the age of twelve would wear the "Tallit Katan", which is the age of accountability in Jewish culture. When we accept Jesus as our Lord and Saviour, we also enter the age of accountability. As we understand, childishly in some instances, what Jesus did on our account, we are ready to praise Him for what He accomplished for our Salvation.

Just like the prayer shawl (Tallit) is worn openly, the "Tallit Katan" is, to some extent, unexposed. It's secret. Only the wearer knows they have put it on. Isn't that the same as meeting with God in private, not shouting what we have done from the rooftops? Not making a show, but quietly and confidentially going about our daily tasks, in the abiding presence of our Heavenly Father. Matthew 6:5–15

Isaiah previously wrote, *"In quietness and confidence shall be your strength"* (Isaiah 30:15a). Our inner strength is gained by placing the *"Garment of Praise"* on first, before we get dressed for the day. It is only when our day becomes hard to bear do we resort to wearing the *"Armour of God"*. We are already protected, but because the battle has gone to another level, we need to stand firm. Ephesians 6:14a

Some things we need to understand about the *"Garment of Praise"*. It is not a get-out-of-jail-free card to be used at will. It's not something you are born with, but it's something you put on yourself. It's no good folded in the drawer or hanging in the closet. It's something you choose to put on. The question could be asked, "Why should I put on the *'Garment of Praise'*?"

Because of what Jesus accomplished on the cross and through His resurrection, receiving the Holy Spirit, the *"Garment of Praise"* is given to you. It is offered to you. It belongs to you. It is available to you. It is always ready to be worn in all circumstances. No one else can wear it for you.

Other people may thank Father God for you, but they can't bring your praise to Father God for you. You need to choose the praise-filled life. True praise is the river that flows out of your heart, and that river is fed by your gratitude to Father God, thankfulness to Father God and praise to Father God.

When you begin each day praising Father God, you will find it almost impossible to harbour anger, bitterness, resentment or hatred. Negative thoughts about others and positive thoughts about Father God cannot coexist. You need to start, maybe slow at first, but you need to start. Let the Holy Spirit fill your heart, and praise will flow out of your mouth:

> *"For out of the abundance of the heart*
> *the mouth speaks."*
>
> Luke 6:45b

As the verse said, *"Out of the abundance of the heart,"* this doesn't mean everything you say will praise Father God, although we would prefer what we say would. Sometimes, the old self comes to the surface and will cause us harm. James gave wise words when he said:

> *"But no man can tame the tongue.*
> *It is an unruly evil, full of deadly poison.*
> *Out of the same mouth*
> *proceed blessings and cursing.*
> *My brethren, these things ought not to be."*
>
> James 3:8; 10

When the battle has overtaken us, we need to confess our failure in true repentance, knowing Father God will forgive, restore, and cleanse not only our mouth, but the thoughts which accompany our thinking and create a clean heart within us. Psalm 51:10–11

Your praise is an invitation to the Holy Spirit to come and indwell you, and when the Spirit of Jesus comes to you, He is going to reign supreme.

Jesus went on to teach, you can't serve Father God and man; in other words, you can't worship money as a god, but we are to make money our servant and use it to meet the needs of others. Jesus left His listeners in no doubt as to their eternal destiny by telling the story of the Rich Man and Lazarus.

Throughout all these parables, Jesus was correcting wrong thinking and the attitude of multiplying things to be used for our own pleasure. Time, health and talents were to be used for others, in extending the kingdom of Father God. Isaiah had some wonderful teaching when he wrote:

> *"Have you not known? Have you not heard?*
> *The everlasting God, the Lord,*
> *the Creator of the ends of the earth,*
> *neither faints nor is weary.*
> *His understanding is unsearchable.*
> *He gives power to the weak,*
> *and to those who have no might He increases strength.*
> *But those who wait on the Lord shall renew their strength;*
> *they shall mount up with wings like eagles.*
> *They shall run and not be weary,*
> *they shall walk and not faint."*
>
> Isaiah 40:28–31

Overview

This passage discusses Jesus' teachings on attitudes, priorities, and the importance of praise in a believer's life.

Jesus Teaching:

- Jesus exposed the wrong motives of religious leaders who prioritised wealth over people's well-being.
- Money should serve people, not become their master.

Prodigal Son & Forgiveness:

- The parable of the prodigal son highlights the Father's readiness to forgive, accept, restore, and rejoice over a lost son's return.

Spiritual Preparation & Praise:

- Believers are encouraged to "get dressed before you get dressed" by spiritually preparing each day, first putting on a *"Garment of Praise"* before the *"Armour of God."*
- The "Tallit Katan" (undergarment) symbolises the personal, inward aspect of praise; the "Tallit" (prayer shawl) symbolises outward spiritual readiness.
- The *"Garment of Praise"* is a voluntary, daily choice, rooted in gratitude and not merely for crisis moments.

Practical Application:

- Genuine praise fosters a positive heart and invites the Holy Spirit's presence, making it difficult to hold negative emotions.
- Jesus warned against serving money and stressed using one's resources for Father God's purposes, not selfish gain.
- Isaiah reminds readers that Father God gives strength to those who wait on Him, encouraging trust and perseverance.
- Regular praise and daily walks with Father God renew strength and keep believers focused.

OTHER LESSONS

Peter

Peter was restored at least twice according to the Gospel accounts. Once at the beginning of his ministry and once in the later stages, with what appears to be turbulence in between. Before we discover the hidden gems in Peter's restorations, let's outline the journey Peter was ordained to fulfil.

About Peter

- Fisherman. Called to discipleship. Matthew 4:18–20; John 1:40-42
- Called as an Apostle. Matthew 10:2–4
- Walked on water. Matthew 14:28–33
- Confessed Christ's deity. Matthew 16:13–19
- Rebuked by Jesus. Matthew 16:21–23
- Witnessed the Transfiguration. Matthew 17:1–8; 2 Peter 1:16–18
- Denied Jesus three times. Matthew 26:69–75
- Commissioned to feed Jesus' flock. John 21:15–17
- Led disciples. Acts 1:15-26
- Preached at Pentecost. Acts 2:1-41

Associated with Jesus

- Peter called to follow Jesus. Matt. 4:18–19
- Peter found tribute money in the fish's mouth. Matt. 17:24–27
- Last Supper, Jesus washed the disciples' feet. John 13:6–7
- Garden of Gethsemane. Cuts off the ear. John 18:25–27
- High Priests' palace. Denial. John 18:10–11
- Peter's remorse. Matt. 26:75
- Peter and John went to the empty tomb. John 20:3–8
- Peter saw Jesus after the Resurrection. John 21:3–17

Ministry after Pentecost

- First missionary journey. Acts 8:14–25
- Second missionary journey. Acts 9:32–11:2
- Third missionary journey. Acts 15:1–14; Galatians 2:11

Peter's Failures

- Refused to follow Jesus. Luke 5:8
- Failed to keep his faith alive. Matthew 14:31
- Failed to understand what Jesus taught. Matthew 15:16
- Failed to understand the meaning of bread. Matthew 16:7
- Peter rebuked Jesus. Matthew 16:23
- Failed to keep quiet at the Transfiguration. Mark 9:5
- Failed to ask Jesus about taxes. Matthew 17:25

- Failed to be humble. Mark 9:34
- Rebuked the little children. Mark 10:13
- Failed to let Jesus wash his feet. John 13:8
- Failed to stay awake in the Garden. Mark 14:37
- Betrays Jesus three times. Matthew 26:75
- Failed to wait for Jesus. John 21:3
- Failed in ministry at Galatia. Galatians 2:11

The Real Peter Revealed

Peter, the rock, the recognised leader and the one who appears first in the lists of disciples in all the Gospels. Mark's gospel is accepted as a record of Peter's recollection, with Mark acting as the scribe. Nothing is kept back, his mistakes, rebukes, and terrible disloyalty, all to show the lengths to which the forgiving love and the recreating grace of Jesus were offered to him.

Peter was a fisherman (Mark 1:16), he was married (1 Corinthians 9:5), and his home was in Capernaum, for it was there Jesus healed his wife's mother. Mark 1:31

As a Galilean, he would have been more anxious for honour than gain, quick-tempered, impulsive, emotional, easily roused by an appeal to adventure, but loyal to the end. Peter was a typical man of Galilee. When you know what a Galilean represented, Jesus was from Nazareth and the exception to the rule.

Within the twelve, Peter was one of the inner circle, James and John the other two. They were present at the raising of

Jairus' daughter (Luke 8:51), the Mount of Transfiguration (Luke 9:28), and in the Garden of Gethsemane (Mark 14:33). It was Peter and John who were sent ahead to prepare for the Passover in Jerusalem. Luke 22:8

Peter stands out as the spokesman, for he asks the meaning of the difficult sayings (Matthew 15:15; Luke 12:41). He asks other questions (Matthew 18:21, 19:27; Mark 11:21 and Mark 13:3). It was Peter who was asked about the taxes (Matthew 17:24), answered about who had touched Jesus (Luke 8:45), and who asked questions of the risen Christ. John 21:20–22

When Jesus asked, *"Who do you say I am?"* it was Peter who answered, *"You are the Christ, the Son of the living God"* (Matthew 16:13–16). When Peter rebuked Jesus for predicting His death, Jesus said, *"Get thee behind me, Satan"* (Matthew 16:22–23), as he did not understand the plan and purpose of Father God. Peter was taught to think of the Son of Man as a celestial figure, clothed in power and glory, dealing out death and destruction to their enemies.

Peter was incapable of making the connection between Jesus and the cross. When walking with Jesus and the other disciples to the Garden of Gethsemane, it was Peter who affirmed unbreakable loyalty to Jesus, in the Garden where he drew his sword and in the courtyard, where his Galilean accent betrayed him, causing him to betray Jesus three times.

It should be said, Peter was first to enter the empty tomb (John 20:6). To whom the risen Christ sent a special message (Mark 16:7) and made a special appearance. 1 Corinthians 15:5

It was Peter who was given the commission to shepherd the flock (John 21:15–17). Peter did many other things, and they are recorded in the Book of Acts. It should be noted about Peter, his greatest characteristic was, however often he might fall and fail, he always recovered his courage and integrity.

Peter's First Restoration

Andrew returned home to Capernaum after John the Baptist was locked up in prison and joined his brother Peter once more, as they worked for Zebedee in the fishing industry.

Jesus was preaching to a great crowd who were pressing closer to Him, so He asked Peter if He could use his boat to teach the crowd. Peter invited Jesus into his boat, and they pulled out a little from the shore. Everyone could hear what Jesus was teaching, including Peter. You could say he was a captive audience.

When Jesus had finished sharing with the crowd, He told Peter to:

> *"Launch out into the deep*
> *and let down their nets for a catch."*
>
> Luke 5:4

Peter explained they had fished all night and caught nothing. Although Peter was a little hesitant, because Jesus asked, he followed His instructions. Peter let down one of his nets and was overcome with the amount of fish caught in the net, so much so, he called his partners James and John, who were washing their nets, to bring their boat and help them.

We are not told whether Jesus helped with the fishing net, but when they reached the shore, Jesus asked Peter to follow Him. Whatever Peter had heard Jesus share from his boat, followed by the enormous catch of fish, cut Peter to the heart as he saw his real self, and *he fell down at Jesus' knees, saying:*

> *"Depart from me,*
>
> *for I am a sinful man,*
>
> *O Lord."*

Luke 5:8

As Peter refused the call of Jesus, his brother Andrew was quick to act, as he'd previously spent time with Jesus when John baptised Jesus. Andrew heard John refer to Jesus as the expected Messiah, the *"Lamb of God who takes away the sin of the world"*, so he went and found his brother and told him:

> *"We have found the Messiah."*

John 1:41

Andrew accompanied Peter as they both came to Jesus. Jesus looked at Simon and said:

> *"You are Simon the son of Jonah.*
> *You shall be called Cephas."*
>
> John 1:42

Jesus again called Peter to follow Him, and this time he accepted. This was the first occasion when Peter received redemption, as he denied the call of Jesus. When Jesus changed Simon to Cephas, his new name or nickname meant a "stone". This was a prophecy about Peter, who would eventually make the confession:

> *"You are the Christ,*
> *the Son of the living God."*
>
> Matthew 16:16

Jesus answered:

> *"And I also say to you that you are Peter,*
> *and on this rock I will build My church,*
> *and the gates of Hades shall not prevail against it."*
>
> Matthew 16:18

Peter, who was Simon, nicknamed Cephas, which meant a stone, made his confession, Jesus was the Son of God, on which Jesus would build the *"Called"*, the "ecclesia", those *"Called"* out of the church to be His kingdom of priests, who would worship Father God in the Holy Jerusalem.

Jesus said Peter's confession was the stone, the rock, the foundation, the cornerstone for the future ministry which Father God had ordained to set up for the redemption of mankind. The Holy Spirit revealed to Peter the eternal plan of Salvation.

Turbulent Times

Peter's faith journey continued when they were on a boat, way out in the sea, tossed about by the waves. Jesus came to them, walking on the water, as if He was going to pass them by (Mark 6:48b), but Peter asked Jesus to prove to him who He was. Peter asked Jesus to let him walk to Him on the water, and Jesus said, *"Come"*. Matthew 14:29a

As Peter climbed out of the boat, his first step onto the water was his first step of faith. Would he be surefooted or would he sink? To his surprise, the sea became firmer with each step he took. With his eyes fixed firmly on Jesus, he walked to Him. Peter was standing face to face with Jesus when the boisterous conditions around him took his focus and attention away from Jesus, and he began to sink. Peter cried out:

> *"Lord, save me!"*
> *And immediately Jesus stretched*
> *out His hand and caught him,*
> *and said to him,*
> *"O you of little faith,*
> *why did you doubt?"*
>
> Matthew 14:30b–31

Peter was face-to-face with Jesus, only an arm's length away, when doubt and fear took control of him.

During Jesus' ministry, accompanied by His disciples, He taught them, the Pharisees, and those gathered many truths, as Jesus imparted the hidden truths not usually taught by the Pharisees. On one occasion, Jesus said:

> *"Hear and understand:*
> *Not what goes into the mouth defiles a man;*
> *but what comes out of his mouth,*
> *this defiles a man."*
>
> Matthew 15:10a–11

The Pharisees understood what Jesus said, but Peter asked Jesus to *"Explain the parable to us"* (Matthew 15:15). Jesus answered Peter and the disciples:

> *"Are you also still without understanding?"*
>
> Matthew 15:16

Jesus uttered the words, *"Hear and understand."* While the Pharisees understood what Jesus said, Peter and the disciples, who were with Jesus every day, did not understand what Jesus taught, as they continually required further explanation from Jesus.

Transfiguration

Peter, along with James and John, was privileged to observe Jesus transfigured, meeting with Moses and Elijah on God's Holy mountain, Mount Hermon. As Peter didn't understand what happened between Jesus and the Prophets, he wanted to build three tabernacles, one for each of the three, but Father God intervened and said:

> *"This is My beloved Son,*
> *in whom I am well pleased.*
> *Hear Him!"*
>
> Matthew 17:5b

When Father God spoke from heaven, Peter fell on his face and was afraid. Jesus had compassion for Him, touched him, and the fear left. Peter, the fisherman, saw Moses and Elijah, men of Father God whom Peter had only heard about in the synagogue scroll readings. Can you imagine what an experience that was for him?

It would appear, Peter, of all the disciples, had the tender love of Jesus leading and teaching him about faith and trust. As there was some confusion with the authorities about them paying tax, Jesus told Peter to take his fishing line, and the first fish he caught would have a coin in its mouth, to take the coin and pay the tax required by the authorities for them both. Matthew 17:24–27

Peter obeyed Jesus and witnessed a miracle, as Jesus taught him a lesson, using a fish and a coin. Peter was to perform miracles himself, as he called on the "Name of Jesus", the "Giver of Miracles" (Acts 3:1–11). Peter also inquired about forgiveness (Matthew 18:21–11), then about the rewards for following Jesus in His ministry. Matthew 19:27

Jesus chose Peter and John to prepare the *"Passover Feast"*, on the *"Day of Preparation"*, for them all to celebrate later that night, after 6 pm, as the Jewish day was 6 pm to 6 pm. Luke 22:7–13

Feet Washing

When Jesus prepared Himself to wash the disciples' feet, it wasn't that they hadn't had their feet washed when they arrived for the *"Passover Feast"*, as the servants who worked for the host would have completed this task. This was different. After the supper, Jesus had shared a teaching about servanthood and the kingdom. Luke 22:25–30

It may seem a curious thing for Peter to ask if Jesus was going to wash his feet, as it would have been very obvious what Jesus was about to do. Maybe Peter was the first and taken a little by surprise. As Peter objected to Jesus' actions, the question to ask is why?

Previously, the disciples had been disputing about who was the greatest, but only amongst themselves (Luke 22:24). No one appeared to think they should be the leader. Jesus shared about a child being the greatest in the kingdom of heaven (Matthew 18:4), that the person should be last of all and a servant of all. Mark 9:35

The disciples were eager for the overthrow of the Romans and hoped Jesus was the long-awaited Messiah to free them from Roman domination. Peter could not imagine Jesus humbling Himself as a servant to complete this task of washing his feet. By his spoken word, Peter affirmed Jesus was the leader and his allegiance to Him when he said:

"You shall never wash my feet!"

John 13:8a

When Jesus told Peter he could not be part of the impending proceedings unless Jesus washed his feet, Peter did a backflip and wanted Jesus to wash his whole body, such was his commitment to the cause. Peter had no understanding of the Spiritual significance of what Jesus' actions meant and the eternal outcome, as Peter was focused on the here and now, the present, not the future.

Peter Warned

Peter was very confident in himself and his loyalty to Jesus. On the way to the Garden of Gethsemane, Jesus shared with the disciples:

> *"All of you will be made to stumble*
> *because of Me this night,*
> *for it is written:*
> *'I will strike the Shepherd,*
> *and the sheep of the flock will be scattered.'*
> *But after I have been raised,*
> *I will go before you to Galilee."*
>
> Matthew 26:31–32

Jesus focused His next remarks on Peter to get his attention:

> *"Simon, Simon!*
> *Indeed, Satan has asked for you,*
> *that he may sift you as wheat.*
> *But I have prayed for you,*
> *that your faith should not fail;*
> *and when you have returned to Me,*
> *strengthen your brethren."*
>
> Luke 22:31–32

All the disciples were listening to Jesus and His warning, as they all swore allegiance to Him (Matthew 26:35b). But Peter replied:

> *"Lord, I am ready to go with You,*
> *both to prison and to death."*

Luke 22:33

Jesus contradicted Peter and tried to help him understand when He predicted:

> *"I tell you, Peter,*
> *the rooster shall not crow this day*
> *before you will deny three times*
> *that you know Me."*

Luke 22:34

Peter wasn't listening or just chose not to understand what Jesus was saying (Luke 22:35–37), as his response was:

> *"Lord, look, here are two swords."*
> *And He said to them;*
> *"It is enough."*

Luke 22:38

Had any of the disciples understood what Jesus shared? One could almost imagine Jesus, knowing what was about to happen, was completely frustrated with the disciples' lack of understanding when He said, *"It is enough."*

Peter did portray some allegiance to Jesus in the altercation between the disciples and those who came to arrest Jesus in the Garden of Gethsamine:

> *"Then Simon Peter, having a sword,*
> *drew it and struck the high priest's servant,*
> *and cut off his right ear."*
>
> *So Jesus said to Peter,*
> *"Put your sword into the sheath.*
> *Shall I not drink the cup*
> *which My Father has given Me?"*

John 18:10–11

Jesus predicted, only a short time before:

> *"All of you will be made to stumble*
> *because of Me this night."*

Matthew 26:31

Matthew records, *"Then all the disciples forsook Him and fled"* (Matthew 26:56b), but in his haste to vacate the garden, Matthew had not observed, *"But Peter followed at a distance."* Luke 22:54

While ten of the disciples had forsaken Jesus and fled, another disciple and Peter, followed Jesus. John, writing many years later, filled in the gaps the other three Gospel writers left out.

> *"Now that disciple*
> *was known to the high priest,*
> *and went with Jesus*
> *into the courtyard of the high priest.*
> *But Peter stood at the door outside.*
>
> *Then the other disciple,*
> *who was known to the high priest,*
> *went out and spoke to her who kept the door,*
> *and brought Peter in."*
>
> John 18:15–16

While the other disciple is not named by John, only one disciple was well known to the high priest, and that was Judas Iscariot. He had orchestrated the arrest terms and received the betrayal money. His father was Simon the Pharisee.

Betrayal

The courageous, loyal, one of the three, Peter, is about to face the real battle, not physically with swords, but verbally with words. The servant girl who kept the door, instructed by Judas, questioned Peter as to his involvement with Jesus, to which Peter replied, *"I am not."* John 18:17

Peter continued to warm himself by the fire, standing with the servants and officers who had made the fire. Noticing Peter, they said,

"You are not also one of His disciples,

are you?"

He denied it and said,

"I am not."

John 18:25

One of the servants of the high priest,

a relative of him whose ear Peter cut off, said,

"Did I not see you in the garden with Him?"

John 18:25a

But Peter said,

"Man, I do not know what you are saying!"

Immediately,

while he was still speaking,

the rooster crowed."

Luke 22:60

And the Lord turned and looked at Peter.
Then Peter remembered the words of the Lord,
how He had said to him,
"Before the rooster crows,
you will deny Me three times."
So Peter went out and wept bitterly.

Luke 22:61–62

As all four gospel accounts are compared, what sets them apart, they are not identical in telling what took place. The question to be asked is, "What did Peter observe? What were the authorities subjecting the One whom Peter knew was the Son of God, the expected Messiah?"

Jesus, who had always shown compassion in all His dealings, was being hit, abused and humiliated. Caiphas had accused Jesus of blasphemy (Matthew 26:65). Peter was helpless to help his friend in these circumstances, and maybe anger, fear, and grief had the upper hand.

Death and Resurrection

Peter and the other disciples watched at a distance as Jesus was crucified (Luke 23:49). Only John ventured to the cross with his aunt Mary and mother Salome, as Jesus had some parting instructions for John. Jesus looked at His mother and said:

> *"Woman, behold your son!"*
> *Then He said to the disciple,*
> *"Behold your mother!"*
>
> John19:26b–27a

The coming days would be a soul-searching time for them all, especially Peter, who may have asked himself over and over, "If only."

Then came Sunday, what a difference three days made. Mary Magdalene was the first to the empty tomb as she arrived very early (John 20:1). Mary had a private encounter with the risen Lord (John 20:11–18). She was joined by the other women, who saw the stone rolled away and ventured inside and saw a young man clothed in a long white robe.

> *But he said to them,*
> *"Do not be alarmed.*
> *You seek Jesus of Nazareth,*
> *who was crucified.*
> *He is reien! He is not here.*
> *See the place where they laid Him.*
> *But go, tell the disciples*
> *and Peter*
> *that He is going before you into Galilee;*

> *there you will see Him,*
> *as He said to you."*

Mark 16:6–7

Saw and Believed

No one was expecting the empty tomb, especially Peter. When the women said they were told to tell the disciples, and Peter was especially named, Peter, along with John, ran to the tomb as they both disbelieved what the women said. When they saw the grave clothes and the napkin in a place by itself, but no body, John believed what they were told by the women.

> *"For as yet they did not know the Scripture,*
> *that He must rise again*
> *from the dead."*

John 20:9

When Jesus did show up in the locked room, the same day as Peter and John had discovered His missing body, belief went out the door (Luke 24:36–49). Not until Jesus brought understanding to the eleven were they able to comprehend the impossible had happened to them, as nothing is impossible to Father God. Mark 10:27

The moments when Jesus was in their presence must have been awkward for the eleven disciples, which did not include

Thomas until eight days later (John 20:26). The two betrayers had walked together and witnessed Jesus' trial by the High Priests and also seen Him crucified. Peter wasn't the only one who felt awkward, but Judas had no idea how to approach Jesus, as he knew Jesus had told him to complete his betrayal mission. John 13:27

At Capernaum

Seven of the disciples travelled to Galilee because on two occasions they were told Jesus would meet them there (Matthew 26:32; 28:7). Patience was not an attribute Peter possessed. When they arrived at Capernium, which was their home base, Jesus was not there to meet them.

Peter became bored with waiting, so he said to the others, *"I am going fishing"*, and the other six disciples agreed (John 21:3a). It had been a turbulent few days, and nothing happened as Peter expected. Jesus crucified, resurrected, coming and going whenever He chose, and now they are in Capernaum, and Jesus is not here. Frustration had taken its toll.

One could almost imagine the whole ministry Peter had experienced was way too much to comprehend. How they were going to overthrow the Romans and rule the then-known world. When Peter said, *"I am going fishing,"* was he saying he quit the disciple band and was going back to being a fisherman once again? Did everyone else feel the same?

At the Seaside

Lake Tiberias was part of the Sea of Galilee, so they obtained a boat and stayed out all night, but caught nothing (John 21:3). A voice came from the shore asking them if they had any food, to which they replied, *"No."*

The disciples were told to:

> *"Cast the net on the right side of the boat,*
> *and you will find some."*
>
> John 21:6a

This suggestion was often given by a person on the shore who could see where the fish were, so the disciples obeyed the advice given.

> *So they cast,*
> *and now they were not able to draw it in*
> *because of the multitude of fish.*
> *Therefore that disciple*
> *whom Jesus loved said to Peter,*
> *"It is the Lord!"*
>
> John 21:6b–7a

What Peter did next, if it wasn't recorded by John, one would find the actions of Peter hard to believe. What was he thinking?

> *"Now when Simon Peter heard*
> *that it was the Lord,*
> *he put on his outer garment*
> *and plunged into the sea."*

John 21:7b

While all the other disciples came in the little boat, dragging the net full of large fish, Peter joined them, soaking wet, in an endeavour to bring the catch to shore. The question to be asked is, "Why would Peter get dressed and jump into the water, not leaving dry clothes to put on afterwards?" Suddenly, Peter's joy turned into despair and misery.

As the previous events of Peter's journey are carefully examined, maybe there is an answer. Some time previous, Peter asked Jesus to let him walk on the sea to Him, and Jesus agreed (Matthew 14:22–33). Did Peter assume this was part of his portfolio, his being able to walk on water? Did Peter not understand, only in the power of Jesus was he able to do what he asked?

Peter's Second Restoration

Jesus knew the heart and thoughts of Peter as He knows our thoughts and actions. Jesus instigated the conversation with Peter as they talked together. Peter was trying to process what happened over the recent weeks, and now he could not even walk on water. Peter was having a pity party, and Jesus knew it. This is revealed in the following verses.

So when they had eaten breakfast, Jesus said to Simon Peter:

*"Simon, son of Jonah,
do you love Me more than these?"
He said to Him,
"Yes, Lord; You know that I love You."
He said to him, "Feed My lambs."
He said to him again a second time,
"Simon, son of Jonah, do you love Me?"
He said to Him,
"Yes, Lord; You know that I love You."
He said to him, "Tend My sheep."
He said to him the third time,
"Simon, son of Jonah, do you love Me?"
Peter was grieved
because He said to him the third time,
"Do you love Me?"
And he said to Him,
"Lord, You know all things;
You know that I love You."
Jesus said to him, "Feed My sheep."*

John 21:15–17

To understand the essence of the conversation Jesus had with Peter, the Greek words referring to *"Love"* need to be considered to receive the impact of what was being conveyed in their conversation. Let us share the reading with the Greek words "Agape" and "Phileo". "Phileo" refers to the love between close friends. "Agape" refers to the love Father God has for His own, unconditional, sacrificial, serves others with humility, selfless, which makes it the highest form of love.

"Simon, son of Jonah,

do you <u>Agape</u> Me more than these?"

He said to Him,

"Yes, Lord; You know that I <u>Phileo</u> You."

He said to him, "Feed My lambs."

He said to him again a second time,

"Simon, son of Jonah, do you <u>Agape</u> Me?"

He said to Him,

"Yes, Lord; You know that I <u>Phileo</u> You."

He said to him, "Tend My sheep."

He said to him the third time,

"Simon, son of Jonah, do you only <u>Phileo</u> Me?"

Peter was grieved

because He said to him the third time,

"Do you <u>Phileo</u> Me?"

And he said to Him,
"Lord, You know all things;
You know that I <u>Phileo</u> You."
Jesus said to him, "Feed My sheep."

Jesus asked Peter twice if he was committed to Him and the future Father God had planned for him, but Peter replied three times, he was only a friend of Jesus. Had Peter just betrayed Jesus for a second time? Peter was grieved, embarrassed; his true inner heart feelings exposed.

Peter immediately saw John near him and tried to take the focus off himself and place it on John. If we didn't know better, one could think we were reading the story about Adam passing the blame to Eve, who blamed the serpent. Does anyone take responsibility for their actions?

Jesus knew Peter's heart. He was about to be restored, knowing in the days ahead, Peter would be bold and forthright, once the power of the Holy Spirit came upon him and possessed him. Jesus directed His words, which impacted Peter and brought restoration when He said:

"You follow Me."

John 21:22b

Jesus did not make a suggestion to Peter, but gave him a command.

This could be the end of Peter's restoration, but are there some details hidden in the background yet to be discovered? We need to revisit the spoken words Jesus previously said to Peter:

> *"Simon, Simon!*
> *Indeed, Satan has asked for you,*
> *that he may sift you like wheat.*
> *But I have prayed for you,*
> *that your faith should not fail;*
> *and when you have returned to Me,*
> *strengthen your brethren."*
>
> Luke 22:31–32

Sifted Like Wheat

Two questions occurred to me. The first is, "Why did Satan choose Peter to sift?" As Peter's life is examined, we notice he was the only disciple to refuse Jesus when called. Peter was selected to be one of the three to accompany Jesus on various occasions; the other two were His cousins. Did this create some pride issues for Peter as he was chosen above the rest?

Peter confessed Jesus was the Christ, but also used by Satan to disagree with Jesus, as Jesus recognised Satan's influence and told Satan to get behind Him. Was Peter more susceptible to satanic influence than the others? Was the fact Peter became the accepted leader amongst the disciples another pride issue, speaking out at the *"Transfiguration"*, rebuked by Father God instead of remaining silent?

Satan had already sifted Judas Iscariot into the betrayal of Jesus; was Peter the next choice, as he looked at the remaining disciples? Was he an easier target than the others? Would he succumb to temptation because he was weaker than the others? Whatever the reason, Father God sanctioned the sifting of Peter.

As I reread the verses, my attention was drawn to the words *"Sift you like wheat"*. The second question to be asked is, "What was the process in Jesus' day of sifted wheat?" In biblical times, sifting wheat involved a process of:

- ***"Threshing"***, to separate the good grain from the chaff, dirt, and stones.
- ***"Winnowing"***, where the mixture was tossed into the air, and the wind would blow the lighter chaff away, allowing the heavier grain to fall to the ground.
- ***"Sifting"***, where the grain was put into a sieve, shaken, and any remaining impurities were removed.

Jesus continued in His advice to Peter, *"But I have prayed for you, that your faith should not fail."* Satan asked permission from Father God to allow him to sift Peter to test his faith? The only other time I remember Satan being coerced into testing someone was when Father God instigated the conversation about His servant Job, which had nothing to do with faith, but patience. Job 1:8

This time is slightly different as Satan is asking Father God to allow him the opportunity to sift Peter. Will Peter survive the sifting, or will he succumb to the temptations and situations before him? Because Jesus assured Peter, *"But I have prayed for you,"* gave Peter the edge to overcome the situations he would experience. Let us consider the days of sifting given to Peter.

<u>Threshing</u>

Sifting was a process, not a one-time occurrence. Over the weeks to follow, Jesus' warning to Peter meant he would experience several trials challenging his allegiance and belief in Jesus. Satan challenged Peter in the following ways:

- Caused him to sleep in the garden of Gethsamine when he should have been praying. Matthew 26:40
- To flee when Jesus was arrested, but followed at a distance. John 18:15
- To deny Jesus three times. Matthew 26:69–75
- To doubt when told of the Resurrection by the women. Luke 24:12
- To disbelieve when Jesus showed up in the locked room. John 20:19
- Became dispondent when Jesus was not at the Sea of Tiberias. John 21:3

<u>Winnowing</u>

Jesus gave further warning to Peter about the impending situation before him when He said to Peter, after He found him sleeping in the Garden of Gethsemane:

> *"Watch and pray,*
> *lest you enter into temptation.*
> *The spirit indeed is willing,*
> *but the flesh is weak."*
>
> Matthew 26:41

Peter was too sleepy to understand the words *"Watch and pray"* were the keys. Peter was focused physically, not spiritually, and unfortunately, these key words from Jesus fell on deaf ears. Peter's faith in Jesus as the Messiah was weakened day by day. It could appear Satan had the upper hand until the seven disciples ventured to Galilee. Mark 16:7

<u>Sifting</u>
When Peter suggested he was going fishing, it may have been an attempt by Satan to sift Peter further. Peter had passed through a few temptations which tested his faith, but would he fulfil Jesus' command to *strengthen his brethren?* Peter had hit rock bottom when he failed to walk to Jesus (John 21:7), as joy turned into despair and misery.

While nothing is recorded about what Jesus shared with the seven disciples over breakfast, He did supply bread for them while they provided the fish (Matthew 4:4). After the disciples had eaten, the conversation between Jesus and Peter was anything but joyous, as Peter, who had been subjected to so much in faith testing, crumbled in front of his Lord.

Good Grain

Jesus restored Peter to his previous relationship they both enjoyed. As only Jesus could, He applied the healing balm of spiritual forgiveness and understanding to the wounded soul of Peter. The Peter who *"When you have returned to Me, strengthen your brethren"*, was now destined to fulfil his called role of discipleship.

So close yet so far. Peter had travelled with Jesus for just over two years and experienced many miracles, healings, and restorations, but almost at the final post, he faltered, as Satan continued to sift him. Within a couple of weeks, the Holy Spirit would descend on them all, as they would experience the understanding they longed for, and a power unrivalled by anything in the past.

We can learn from the experience of Peter, although we may believe we are infallible at times, and become consumed with our works. Has Satan been allowed to sift each one of us, but except for the "Agape" love of Father God, prevented us from being lost? The words patience, persistence, and perseverance are necessary to ensure the work of Father God is not frustrated.

Overview

Peter was a fisherman called by Jesus to be a disciple and apostle. He is known for his leadership among the disciples and significant moments of faith and failure.

Early Life and Calling

- Fisherman from Galilee.
- Called to discipleship. Matthew 4:18–20
- Renamed Cephas by Jesus. John 1:42

Key Events in Jesus' Ministry

- Walked on water. Matthew 14:28–33
- Confessed Jesus as the Messiah. Matthew 16:16
- Witnessed the Transfiguration. Matthew 17:1-8
- Denied Jesus three times. Matthew 26:69–75

Personal Struggles and Growth

- Peter showed impulsiveness, often needing clarification on Jesus' teachings. Matthew 15:15
- Experienced significant remorse after denying Jesus, leading to deep reflection. Luke 22:61–62
- Demonstrated loyalty but struggled with understanding Jesus' mission. Matthew 16:22–23

Final Restoration

- After the resurrection, Peter was specifically named by the angel. Mark 16:7
- He initially returned to fishing but was reminded of his calling by Jesus. John 21:6
- Jesus' three questions about Peter's love brought Restoration. John 21:15–17

Restoration and Ministry

- After denying Jesus, Peter experienced deep remorse but was restored by Jesus. John 21:15–17
- His later boldness was credited to the Holy Spirit's empowerment at Pentecost. Acts 2:11
- Led the early church, preached at Pentecost, and undertook missionary journeys. Acts 2:14–39

Themes

- Peter's story emphasises human struggle, the need for humility, perseverance under trial, and the transformative power of Jesus' forgiveness, grace and restoration.

Zacchaeus

The redemption story of Zacchaeus, detailed in Luke 19:1–10, is marked by his genuine repentance for past wrongs and his transformation into a new person after encountering Jesus. When Jesus publicly called him out of a tree, Zacchaeus declared he would give half his possessions to the poor and repay four times the amount if he had defrauded anyone

This act of restitution and generosity, along with his new attitude, signified his redemption, as Jesus stated, *"Salvation had come to this house"*.

Several questions need to be asked.

- What do we know about Jericho?
- Who was Zacchaeus, and what did he do?
- How did Jesus know Zacchaeus to call him by name?
- What was the significance of the tree Zacchaeus had climbed?
- Jesus' invitation to Zacchaeus.
- What significance did the actions of Zacchaeus have?
- What is understood by *"Salvation"* in the time of Jesus?

Jericho

Jericho, in the time of Jesus, was situated beautifully, a city of palm trees, and became the priestly city where the religious leaders lived when not fulfilling their duties in Jerusalem. Jericho, a city of history and religion, was a place of privilege. It was a long time since Joshua and the children of Israel fought the battle of Jericho.

Rahab and her family were the only survivors from the children of Israel's assault on their well-fortified city. As Rahab married Salmon of the tribe of Judah, through his bloodline, King David and Bathsheba had four sons. Two of their sons, Solomon and Nathan, through the bloodline of their respective families, continued for about 800 years until Joseph and Mary were chosen by Father God to be the earthly parents of Jesus.

Jericho is one of the earliest continuously inhabited settlements in the world, dating back to around 9000 B.C. This provides evidence of early permanent settlement and the domestication of plants in the Fertile Crescent. Herod the Great built a lavish winter palace in the city of Jericho to escape the cold of Jerusalem.

The Jericho-Jerusalem road was and is one of the main paths across the Judean Desert. Jericho, with its flourishing oasis and many palm trees, was a strategic crossroads in the road network of ancient Palestine. The road leading to and from Jericho, used by merchants, armies, and pilgrims, was important throughout history.

Jesus passed through Jericho on His way to Jerusalem, which was 785 meters above sea level, where Jericho was 276 meters below sea level. The distance between was about 40 kilometres, as you would walk uphill from Jericho towards the Mount of Olives, passing through Bethany, which was on the east side and approximately 826 meters above sea level. The road descended into the Kidron Valley about 450 meters below sea level, then climbed again to the heights of Jerusalem.

Zacchaeus

While no direct lineage or tribe is recorded, Jesus referred to Zacchaeus as a *"son of Abraham"*, which aligned him with a Jewish past. He was the chief tax collector, which meant he was in charge of all the tax collectors, making him even more reviled by the Jewish people who lived in Jericho, a prominent and wealthy town in biblical times.

The Jewish people despised tax collectors because they often worked for the Roman authorities and were known for their corrupt practices, overcharging and enriching themselves at the expense of others. Zacchaeus' wealth came with a social cost, as in the eyes of his community, he was seen as a sinner and an outsider.

Jesus and Zacchaeus

As Jesus called Zacchaeus by name, and Zacchaeus wanted to see Jesus, both had prior knowledge of each other. This was no chance meeting or coincidence. We need to ask the question, why did Zacchaeus want to see Jesus? It wasn't because of tax evasion, as we are told Jesus paid His taxes. Matthew 17:24–27

Zacchaeus wanted to see Jesus due to a deep, spiritual, divine, inner "thirst" and a desire for something more than his wealth offered. A curiosity about the man who was rumoured to be the Messiah, and perhaps a longing for friendship.

Zacchaeus was determined to overcome his height and the community's disapproval of him, to get a glimpse of Jesus, indicating a genuine yearning for change and spiritual fulfilment. Zacchaeus' eagerness to see Jesus suggested a deeper, innate desire to connect with Father God, even if he didn't fully understand at the time.

As Jesus travelled, many people were curious about Him and the miracles He performed. Zacchaeus most likely heard about Jesus and wanted to see for himself who this influential figure was. He may have been drawn to Jesus, who was known to interact with and accept people others rejected, including tax collectors, a profession that included one of Jesus' own disciples. Matthew 9:9

Despite his wealth, Zacchaeus may have felt empty or unfilled, as his extreme effort to see Jesus, which included climbing a tree, pointed to a genuine desire for change and something deeper than material possessions could provide. The very act of seeking Jesus, overcoming obstacles, and later offering restitution suggested he was ready to change his life and become a part of Father God's family.

A Tree Climber

Jesus was walking through the city of Jericho and looked up into a Sycamore tree. One could guess He was looking for fig mulberries, as this is the fruit the Sycamore tree produces. If you want to know more about this tree and fruit, you will need to read Amos, because he was not only a shepherd but a keeper of Sycamore Trees.

> *"I was no prophet,*
> *nor was I a son of a prophet,*
> *but I was a sheepbreeder*
> *and a tender of sycamore fruit."*

Amos 7:14

The Bible tells us Jesus saw Zacchaeus.

> *And when Jesus came to the place,*
> *He looked up and saw him, and said to him,*
> *"Zacchaeus, make haste and come down,*
> *for today I must stay at your house."*
> *So, he made haste and came down*
> *and received Jesus joyfully.*

Luke 19:5–6

To everyone's surprise, Jesus stopped, looked up at Zacchaeus and talked directly to him. This public invitation shocked the crowd, as to why Jesus would choose to associate with someone as sinful as Zacchaeus? But Jesus' actions reflected His mission to seek out the lost sheep of Israel.

Jesus was in the presence of ninety-nine sheep that needed, as they thought, no repentance, as their focus was on Jesus, but Jesus was looking for the lost sheep. Part of His mission was to seek and save those lost to the kingdom, and He saw Zacchaeus up in the Sycamore tree branches.

A Symbol of Israel

Is there a deeper lesson about the Sycamore Tree and its fruit? Amos' job was a shepherd as well as a tender of sycamore fruit, whose job was to puncture the fig to let the fly inside out; if left, the fruit turned bad.

The observation could be made of what Jesus saw as He looked into the tree. Did Jesus see a ripe fig mulberry required to be punctured, to let out the bad? Jesus, the Good Shepherd, saw and recognised the hidden person, punctured the heart, to release the bad, and revealed the real Zacchaeus.

Did Jesus see the lost sheep as it had strayed and became "cast down" by his circumstances? Did Jesus understand, having lost the coin of belonging to his own people and Salvation, just like the prodigal, He wrapped His arms of protection around him and returned him safe to his original position in front of the crowd?

Redemption

Zacchaeus' response to Jesus was immediate and heartfelt as he welcomed Jesus joyfully into his home. This act of hospitality marked the beginning of his transformation, as during the meal Jesus shared with Zacchaeus, he made a bold declaration:

> *"Look, Lord,*
> *I give half of my goods to the poor;*
> *and if I have taken anything from anyone*
> *by false accusation,*
> *I restore fourfold."*

Luke 19:8

So, what brought Zacchaeus to this decision? What do we know about this man? He was the chief tax collector, he was rich and also a short man. Vertically challenged, so to speak. He was into tree climbing. He received Jesus joyfully.

He was branded a sinner by the crowd. He had the gift of generosity. He was a *"son of Abraham"*. Ah, hold on. Something doesn't seem to sit right here. He had the gift of generosity. He was a *"son of Abraham"*. Was it the tall poppy syndrome? How we love to pull down those people who have made it for any reason, good or bad.

Let's revisit what has happened in the story. Here we have a man who has given away half of his possessions and is now inviting people to line up and take what he has left. As the chief tax collector, this would not happen overnight, and there would be literally thousands he would have dealt with. He could say with some confidence, I have never cheated anyone out of anything they rightfully needed to pay.

I seem to recall Matthew was at the receipt of custom, a customs officer, which the Jews considered a profession worse than ordinary tax collection, but nobody said he was a thief or a robber, and Matthew eventually wrote one of the gospels. Is it recorded during Matthew's time with Jesus, did anyone accuse him of wrong dealings?

When you look at the disciples Jesus chose, knowing what we know about their backgrounds and faults, would you have chosen them? It appears to me, all these years, Zacchaeus had a pretty raw deal from everyone, and Jesus put it right.

This is the classic example of the perceived view.

1. First, there is the person whom everyone sees. The crowd said he is a sinner.
2. Then there is the view he portrayed of himself. I am the Chief Tax Collector. Zacchaeus had a position to uphold.
3. Then there is the real person, the one, very few people ever see.

How Zacchaeus responded to Jesus reflected true repentance as Zacchaeus not only acknowledged any wrongdoing but also took steps to make amends. As Zacchaeus had not frauded anyone, His actions aligned with the Jewish law regarding restitution (Leviticus 25), showing his sincere desire to live a righteous life.

In the case of the Rich Young Ruler, his riches meant everything to him (Matthew 19:22), but in the case of Zacchaeus, covetousness had no part in him, as he immediately gave away half of his possessions to the poor. Zacchaeus said:

"If I have taken anything

from anyone by false accusation,

I restore fourfold."

Luke 19:8

Zacchaeus was declaring, not only were his possessions opened to scrutiny, but also his wealth and money. Just like Matthew, who was able to close up his books and straightway follow Jesus, knowing there was nothing fraudulent committed against any person, Zacchaeus was able, with confidence, to do the same with a clear conscience.

Zacchaeus may have been a tax collector, but he was still a *"son of Abraham"*, who was entitled to the promises available to him as a descendant. Because he honoured the Father, Father God brought the increase and blessed him. Because he, unlike the others who pointed the finger and found fault with him, those who were also sinners, was honoured and blessed in his dealings.

Salvation

In the Old Testament, Salvation was achieved by God's grace through faith in Him and His promises, including the coming Messiah, and was foreshadowed by the sacrificial system, the Passover lamb, circumcision, and other covenant ordinances.

Jesus knew the repentant Zacchaeus was saved, rescued from the bondage, power, guilt, and penalty of his sin. The community should no longer consider Zacchaeus a sinner, as Jesus told the crowd, *"Today salvation has come to this house."* Luke 19:9a

Since Zacchaeus was so hated by his fellow Jews, they probably said he wasn't a "real" Jew, so Jesus wanted everyone to know Zacchaeus was a *"son of Abraham"*, both by genetics and by faith, because he joyfully received Jesus.

As Jericho was a Levitical city, the priests of Jericho could have condemned Zacchaeus and called on him to give to the poor. But after meeting Jesus, such a sacrifice was done joyfully. Luke 18:9–14

Jesus' last remarks were:

> *"The Son of Man has come*
> *to seek and to save*
> *that which was lost."*

Luke 19:10

Jesus explained why He sought and extended friendship to a sinner like Zacchaeus, as Jesus came precisely to save people like Zacchaeus. Zacchaeus believed in Jesus, and as a true *"son of Abraham"*, he had the faith in God Abraham had.

Even though Zacchaeus sought Jesus, it turns out he was the one who was lost, and Jesus sought him. Zacchaeus was lost to religion, lost to his community, lost to whatever Jewish friends he might have, but not lost to Father God. As the story of his Salvation unfolds, his seeking Jesus turned out to be the result of Jesus' first seeking him.

The story of Zacchaeus is a beautiful example of how encountering Jesus changes lives. From a despised tax collector to a joyful, repentant follower of Jesus, Zacchaeus' transformation reminds us no one is beyond the reach of Father God's grace. His story invites us to seek Jesus with determination, respond to His call with repentance, and live a life worthy of His calling.

Overview

Zacchaeus' story in Luke 19:1-10 illustrates his transformation from a despised tax collector to a joyful follower of Jesus through genuine repentance.

Jericho

- Jericho is a historical city in the Bible, known for its palm trees and as a centre of privilege.
- It is one of the oldest inhabited cities, dating back to 9000 B.C.
- Herod the Great built a winter palace there.

Zacchaeus

- Zacchaeus was the chief tax collector, despised for working with the Romans.
- He was seen as a sinner and an outsider despite being a *"son of Abraham"*.
- His wealth came with social stigma from the Jewish community.

Encounter with Jesus

- Zacchaeus wanted to see Jesus due to a deep spiritual yearning.
- He climbed a sycamore tree to overcome his height disadvantage and crowd disapproval.
- Jesus called him by name, indicating a personal connection.
- This surprised the crowd as Jesus chose to associate with Zacchaeus.

Significance of the Tree

- The sycamore tree symbolises Zacchaeus' desire for change and spiritual fulfilment.
- Jesus' invitation to Zacchaeus reflects His mission to save the lost.

Redemption

- Zacchaeus joyfully welcomed Jesus into his home, marking the beginning of his transformation.
- He pledged to give half his possessions to the poor and repay any he defrauded fourfold.
- His actions demonstrated true repentance and a desire to live righteously.

Understanding Salvation

- Salvation in Jesus' time was linked to faith in Father God and His promises.
- Jesus affirmed Zacchaeus' Salvation, emphasising he was a true *"son of Abraham"*.
- Zacchaeus' story illustrates no one is beyond Father God's grace.

Thomas

In the Bible, the Apostle Thomas is known as "Doubting Thomas" because he refused to believe the other apostles when they said Jesus had risen from the dead until he could physically see and touch the wounds of the resurrected Jesus. His story highlights the journey from scepticism to faith. His faith was restored when Jesus appeared to him and allowed him to touch His wounds, culminating in Thomas' declaration, *"My Lord and my God!"*

The concept of "Redemption" refers to humanity's Salvation through Jesus Christ's sacrifice and Resurrection, an occurrence Thomas eventually accepted after he overcame his disbelief. He was known for his earnestness, courage, and his crucial role in the post-Resurrection appearances and the commission of the apostles.

Who is Thomas?

When the disciple Thomas is mentioned, what first comes to mind? The Doubter. Why? There are four references to Thomas.

- Urging disciples to go with Jesus even if it meant death. John 11:16
- Spoke on behalf of the disciples. John 14:5
- See the nail prints, etc. John 20:24–29
- Numbered among those disciples going fishing. John 21:2–3

Firstly, we should say Thomas was a man of courage. He appeared to be a pessimist; however, by accompanying Jesus to Jerusalem, he was prepared to face death as an acceptable option. John 11:16

Secondly, Thomas became bewildered by what Jesus said as he didn't understand where He was going. He asked a question, even though the answer left him somewhat confused. John 14:5

Thirdly, Thomas needed to see to believe; his desire for visible proof was recalled throughout history. His devastation at Jesus' death could only be cured by visible proof, as no one had ever survived the ordeal Jesus went through and came back to life. Thomas required to see the risen Jesus to believe in the Resurrection.

Fourthly, Thomas became a man of devotion and faith when Jesus invited him to touch His nail prints and spear-pierced side (John 20:27), then breathed out the greatest confession of faith in the New Testament, *"My Lord, and My God"* (v28). Jesus never criticised a person for wanting to be sure.

Only when we truly believe can we make His message truly known to others. Thomas was a loner and required solitude to compose himself, but when he returned to the fellowship of believers, found his answer, numbered with the disciples by the Sea of Galilee. John 21:1–14

Thomas was never a doubter; he did not believe, and this is not doubt. To define doubt, it's a feeling of uncertainty or lack of conviction. There was no uncertainty in the mind of Thomas; no one survived crucifixion.

Thomas' Past

Jesus was about halfway through His ministry when He held the night of prayer to select the remaining five disciples. Jesus called Philip, who told Nathaniel about Jesus, and they became followers in Jesus' Judean ministry. Jesus, in His Galilean ministry, called Peter, Andrew, James, John and Matthew. After the night of prayer, Jesus called Thomas, James the son of Alphaeus, Thaddaeus, Simon the Zealot, and Judas Iscariot.

By the time Jesus called His twelve disciples, the growing sentiment He was the expected Messiah, who would free the Jewish race from the oppression of the Romans, was accepted by the majority of the people. It would appear Thomas had his reservations about Jesus' identity, but as Jesus chose him, he accepted the call to follow Jesus.

Observations

When Jesus sent out the twelve in ministry (Luke 9:1–6), He gave them power and authority over demons and to cure diseases. Many heard the gospel preached to them, and everywhere, people were healed. Thomas had no problem trusting Jesus, as he saw the miracles, and this reinforced the fact, Jesus was the expected Messiah.

Thomas was present but not involved in many of the miracles and healings Jesus performed. He was more of an observer who kept his thoughts to himself, as he was looking for the warrior Messiah most people expected. Thomas is first featured when Jesus is going to raise Lazarus from the dead.

The situation in Jerusalem concerning Jesus was volatile, and the disciples were afraid of the consequences, except for Thomas, who said:

> *"Let us also go,*
> *that we may die with Him."*
>
> John 11:16a

Thomas was ready for the overthrow of the Romans, and even if he was called to die, then let it be. He rallied the other disciples to patriotism, as this is why they joined and followed Jesus. Thomas called them to the complete sacrifice they answered to when Jesus called them, knowing the day would arrive when their sacrifice was required if necessary, and this could be the day.

Uncertainty

On many occasions when Jesus spoke to the disciples, they did not understand what He said, as the Holy Spirit hadn't been given to them. Jesus and the disciples celebrated the *"Passover"*, Judas had left to carry out something Jesus told him to do, and Jesus was teaching them all about some new covenant which involved Him and His preparing a place for them.

Thomas was confused about where Jesus was planning to go, although He told them they knew where He was going and they should go the same way. As this baffled Thomas, he said:

> *"Lord,*
>
> *we do not know where You are going,*
>
> *and how can we know the way?"*
>
> John 14:5

To Thomas as well as Philip (John 14:8), Jesus was talking in riddles. So many questions were answered with more riddles, but this was Jesus, the One they chose to follow. Like so much in the past Jesus said and taught, was this any different? Thomas required clarification about what Jesus was saying. Did he miss something?

The Confrontation

The hour was late, and the celebration had finished, but Jesus decided they should leave, so they all followed Him, as on many occasions, had no idea where they were going or what Jesus had in mind. As they walked together, Jesus told them:

> *"All of you will be made to stumble*
> *because of Me this night, for it is written:*
> *'I will strike the Shepherd,*
> *and the sheep will be scattered'.*
> *But after I have been raised,*
> *I will go before you to Galilee."*
>
> Mark 14:27

One could imagine Thomas thinking to himself, *More riddles?* They crossed the Kidron Brook and made their way up the side of the mountain to the Garden of Gethsemane. Jesus often frequented this place, so while three of the disciples continued with Jesus, after being told by Jesus to pray, Thomas fell fast asleep, as it had been a long day and the meal was very satisfying.

Thomas suddenly awoke when the soldiers arrived with Judas, as they came to arrest Jesus. When an altercation took place between Jesus and the soldiers, Jesus requested His disciples be let go. The hour arrived, but their hearts failed them, as *they all forsook Him and fled.* Mark 14:50

Crucifixion

The brave hearts somehow lost heart, despite the disciples all vowing not to betray Jesus. Nothing more is recorded about Thomas until Jesus is being crucified, when we are told:

> *"But all His acquaintances,*
> *and the women*
> *who followed Him from Galilee,*
> *stood at a distance, watching these things."*
>
> Luke 23:49

Unbelief to Belief

After some time passed, Thomas would once again join the other disciples in the locked room, and they were adamant they had seen the Lord. Thomas, who was in total disbelief such a thing could happen, as he had witnessed Jesus die, said:

> *"Unless I see in His hands the print of the nails,*
> *and put my finger into the print of the nails,*
> *and put my hand into His side,*
> *I will not believe."*
>
> John 20:25

Thomas' words do not imply doubt as he said, *"I will not believe."* He did not believe what the disciples were saying.

Had what they seen been a ghost, similar to when Jesus came walking to them on the water? Matthew 14:26

Thomas was processing the occurrences over the past days, and Jesus' appearing to the disciples did not seem possible. Thomas refused to believe. He didn't doubt the resurrection; he rejected it entirely and claimed he would never believe without physically touching the risen Jesus.

Eight days had passed since Jesus stood in the locked room with the eleven disciples, and the two followers who had travelled to Emmaus (Luke 24:36), but Thomas was not present for Jesus' appearance (Mark 16:14). As the twelve disciples were all present in the locked room, Jesus stood in their midst, and said:

"Peace be with you!"
Then He said to Thomas,
"Reach your finger here,
and look at My hands;
and reach your hand here,
and put it into My side.
Do not be unbelieving,
but believing."

John 20:27

Because Thomas saw with his eyes and felt the wounds Jesus sustained, his disbelief turned to belief, as he said:

"My Lord and my God!"

John 20:28

Jesus knew Thomas needed to believe, and He provided the evidence. Jesus lovingly met Thomas at the exact point of his need and then guided him back to faith. Thomas never doubted; he did not believe the impossible could be possible. Jesus went on to minister to Thomas as He said:

"Thomas, because you have seen Me,
you have believed.
Blessed are those who have not seen
and yet have believed."

John 20:29

From disbelief to faith serves as an example of the transformative power of encountering the risen Jesus. Thomas demanded physical proof of Jesus' wounds and, upon receiving it, explicitly acknowledged Jesus' divinity.

Sustained Belief

A few days passed, and Thomas was numbered with those who met Jesus in Galilee at the Sea of Tiberius. He was one of seven who answered the call of Jesus to meet Him there and witnessed the miraculous power exhibited by Jesus, the Son of God. All belief was sustained when Jesus invited them to eat breakfast.

> *"None of the disciples dare ask Him,*
>
> *'Who are You?'*
>
> *knowing it was the Lord."*
>
> John 21:12

Right before Jesus gave the "Great Commission" and then ascended to the Father, Matthew reported the eleven disciples worshipped Jesus, *but some doubted* (Matthew 28:16). They did believe Jesus had risen from the dead, but some harboured doubts. Given Thomas was firm in his belief, I suspect he was not one of the apostles who Matthew reported as doubting. It would appear other apostles were greater doubters than Thomas.

The final mention of Thomas is in Acts 1:13, where he is listed among the disciples who returned from the Mount of Olives after the Ascension to wait for the promise. He is in the upper room prayer meeting with all the others as:

> *"These all continued with one accord*
>
> *in prayer and supplication,*
>
> *with the women and*
>
> *Mary the mother of Jesus,*
>
> *and with His brothers."*
>
> Acts 1:14

The account of Thomas deals with unbelief, not doubt. Thomas was expecting the prophesied Messiah, and through his time spent with Jesus, witnessed miracles to verify Jesus' power and identity. Believing in Jesus was the only appropriate response to all the previous truths Thomas saw. Thomas' life reminds us that Father God gives life when we believe Jesus is the Messiah.

Overview

This text examines the biblical portrayal of Thomas, often labelled as "Doubting Thomas," emphasising his journey from disbelief in Jesus' resurrection to a profound declaration of faith.

Thomas's Journey:

- Four biblical references show Thomas as courageous, honest about his confusion, and required evidence.
- Demonstrated willingness to die for Jesus and demanded clarification when confused. John 11:16, 14:5
- Known for his refusal to believe Jesus had risen until he saw proof. John 20:25
- His unbelief turned to belief only when he saw and touched the risen Jesus. John 20:24–29
- After his encounter, he affirmed Jesus' divinity and joined other disciples in Galilee. John 21

Character and Significance:

- Thomas was not a persistent doubter but someone who refused to believe without evidence.
- He was present in critical moments but often reserved, attributed his questions and expectations of a warrior Messiah.
- His insistence on evidence served to reinforce the reality and impact of the Resurrection for early Christian faith.

Ultimate Legacy:

- Thomas' example highlights the difference between doubt and disbelief; he rejected the Resurrection until faced with direct evidence.
- He later became strong in faith, present at key post-Resurrection appearances and prayer meetings.
- The narrative positions Thomas as a model for honest inquiry and the potential for deep faith following initial scepticism.

Cleansed and Restored

The Bible shared another story of Redemption, but with a twist, as the redemption was to do with healing. The "Woman with the Issue of Blood" was redeemed by her faith, which led to physical and spiritual healing by Jesus, who declared, *"Your faith has made you well"*.

Suffering from a chronic bleeding disorder for twelve years, she was considered ritually unclean and an outcast under Jewish Law. Her act of touching Jesus' garment in faith brought immediate healing, and her encounter with Jesus restored her, providing physical healing, ending her isolation, and affirming a right relationship with the Father through her faith.

To understand the implications, the depth of knowledge and devotion portrayed by the unknown woman will be dealt with in the following ways:

- Preceding Events
- The Incident
- About the woman
- Jesus' Prayer Shawl
- Jesus' reaction
- Restoration

Preceding Events

On another occasion, the disciples witnessed the healing of a demon-possessed man named Legion in the country of the Gadarenes opposite Galilee. While the local people associated with Legion were hostile to Jesus, when Jesus and the disciples returned to Capernaum, the multitude welcomed Jesus, as they were waiting for Him. Luke 8:40

The Incident

One could imagine the disciples bathing in the glory when, out of nowhere, Jesus asked a question:

> *"Who touched me?"*
>
> Luke 8:45

While we are told the disciples tried to make excuses, Jesus said the words:

> *"Somebody touched Me,*
> *for I perceived power going out from Me."*
>
> Luke 8:46

One could only try to imagine the disciples' thoughts when they witnessed a woman, trembling, fall at the feet of Jesus, and confessed the reason and how she was healed immediately. Jesus said to her:

> *"Daughter, be of good cheer,*
> *your faith has made you well.*
> *Go in peace."*

Luke 8:48

The disciples and the crowd saw a woman with a sickness, but Jesus called her a daughter. What did Jesus previously say about family?

> *"My mother and My brothers are these*
> *who hear the word of God and do it."*

Luke 8:21

The questions to be asked are, "What did she do, and why did Jesus call her a daughter?"

About the Woman

The woman was a Jew and knew the scriptures of their day, as she probably memorised them. She knew the prophet Malachi wrote how the Jewish people could recognise the true Messiah. Let me share with you the following verse.

> *"But to you who fear My name*
> *the Sun of Righteousness*
> *shall arise with healing in His wings."*

Malachi 4:2a

The woman suffered from an unstoppable bleeding for twelve years, a condition that made her ritually unclean and forced her to live in isolation. The Levitical Law stated:

> *"If a woman has a discharge,*
> *and the discharge from her body is blood,*
> *she shall be set apart seven days;*
> *and whoever touches her*
> *shall be unclean until evening."*
>
> Leviticus 15:19

Although the law was often abused with wrong interpretations, this law was set in place by Father God to protect women, to set them apart from the weekly duties of housework and caring for children, amongst other things, the women were to carry out. The Father cares for women as He does for all, including proper rest and recovery.

Despite seeing many doctors, the woman's condition worsened, leaving her desperate after having spent all her resources. Hearing about Jesus, she came to believe, simply touching the hem of His garment would heal her.

This woman had twelve years of no hugs, no kisses, or shared meals. She couldn't go out in public, socialise with the other women to draw water from the well, or venture out to worship at the synagogue or temple. Nothing for twelve years. Twelve years without human contact would take a toll on anyone's emotional state.

Understanding the culture of the Jewish community, if a person suffered in any way, the affliction was an outward sign of inward (hidden) sin. We know she was a woman of faith. How do we receive faith? By hearing the Word of God. Romans 10:17

Jesus stopped and asked who touched Him. Can you imagine the fear this woman felt when Jesus drew attention to what happened? We need to keep two things in mind:

- This woman hadn't touched or been touched in years.
- Jesus only did and said what the Father in Heaven told Him to do or say. John 5:19–20

Father God saw this woman still cowering and trying to hide, because of her emotional wounds, only the Father could see; feelings of shame, fear, and anxiety hadn't been transformed yet. Father God loved her so much, He couldn't let her walk away with emotional wounds still festering. So Jesus immediately responded, stopped everything and addressed the situation.

The bravest thing this woman did was step forward in front of everyone, fall at the feet of Jesus, and confess she was a lawbreaker. As she'd broken the Jewish Law, the people could have stoned her to death. Amidst the crowd, she reached out and touched Jesus' garment. Immediately, her bleeding stopped, and she felt the suffering end.

The Prayer Shawl

When Jesus was walking through the crowd, He was wearing His *"Prayer Shawl"*. When a Jew sought a private place to pray, they would place the prayer shawl over their head, forming wings. Tassels were attached to the edge or hem of the garment. She knew the true Messiah would have healing power in the fringe of his *"Prayer Shawl"*; all she was required to do was touch the fringe, and she would be healed.

About the Prayer Shawl

The "Tallit" is a *"Prayer Shawl"*, the most authentic Jewish garment. It is a rectangular-shaped piece of linen or wool with special fringes called "Tzitzit" on each of the four corners. The purpose of the garment is to hold the "Tzitzit" and acts as a head covering for prayer. The word "Tallit" isn't originally Hebrew and does not appear in the Bible; rather, other words meaning robe or garment are paired with words meaning tassel or fringe to indicate the proper attire.

The King James version says, *"Bid them that they make them fringes in the borders of their garments"* (Numbers 15:38). The word *"borders"* translated is "kanaph", which meant wing, extremity, edge, winged, border, corner (of garment). This was required on the four corners of the clothing of every Jewish male in accordance with Father God's instructions.

In Jesus' day, Jewish men wore a simple tunic both at home and at work. When appearing in public, they would cover their tunic with a large rectangular cloth draped over the shoulders and fell to the ankles. This cloth served as protection from cold and rain. Hanging from the end of each of its four corners (wings) was a "Tzitzit" in obedience to the biblical command. In biblical times, Jewish men wore the *"Prayer Shawl"* all the time, not just at prayer.

Tal-ith contains two Hebrew words: "Tal" meaning *tent*, and "ith" meaning *little*. Thus, you have "Little Tent". Each Israelite man had his own "little tent". About two and a half million Jews could not fit into the tent of meeting (Exodus 33:7) set up in the Old Testament. Each man was given his own *"Prayer Shawl"* or "Tallit" as their own private sanctuary, where they could meet with Father God.

They would pull it up over their head, the "Diadem" forming the crown of the garment, outstretching their arms, making a tent, where they would begin to chant, sing their Hebrew songs, and call upon Father God. It was intimate, private, and set apart from everyone else, enabling them to totally focus upon Father God, as this was their prayer closet!

Let me share with you some verses from the Psalms:

> *He who dwells in the secret place*
> *of the Most High shall abide*
> *under the shadow(protection) of the Almighty.*
> *I will say of the Lord,*
> *"He is my refuge and my fortress;*

> *My God, in Him I will trust.*
> *Surely, He shall deliver you*
> *from the snare of the fowler*
> *and from the perilous pestilence.*
> *He shall cover you with His feathers,*
> *and under His wings you shall take refuge;*
> *His truth shall be your shield and buckler."*
>
> Psalms. 91:1–4

Did you notice the word *"wings"*? With this understanding in mind, an ancient Jew under the *"Prayer Shawl"* could be said to be dwelling in the secret place of the Most High and under His wings.

Let me draw your attention to another verse of scripture.

> *"But to you who fear My name,*
> *the Sun of Righteousness*
> *shall arise with healing in His wings."*
>
> Malachi 4:2a

Let me recall a previous reading. *"Suddenly, a woman who had a flow of blood for twelve years came from behind and touched the hem (Tzitzit) of His garment (Tallit). For she said to herself, 'If only I may touch His garment (Tallit), I shall be made well'."* Matthew 9:20–21

When you realise the significance of this concept to the first-century Hebraic mind, it became clear why this woman was healed instantly. She was expressing her faith in Jesus as the *"Sun of Righteousness"* with, *"But unto you that fear my name shall the Sun of Righteousness arise with healing in His wings."* Malachi 4:2

Earlier in this document, I mentioned the "Diadem" was the crown of this garment, placed on your head and forming the little tent as you raised your arms. Edward Perronet (1726–1792) penned the words of a song. Let me share the first and last verses with you.

All hail the power of Jesus' name!
Let angels prostrate fall;
Bring forth the Royal Diadem and crown Him,
crown Him, crown Him, crown Him,
Lord of all!

O that with yonder sacred throng
we at His feet may fall,
Join in the everlasting song and crown Him,
crown Him, crown Him, crown Him,
Lord of all!

Public Domain

For so many years, I have sung these words with great gusto, but never understood the power and meaning contained in this song and its verses.

Jesus' Reaction

What did Jesus do about her actions? Instead of condemning her, He took time and acknowledged her. He called her a daughter, publicly claiming her as His own. I love how the KJV records this verse: *"He told her, 'Your faith had made you whole; go in peace'."* Not cured, and not just healed, but whole!

The disciples and the crowd saw a woman who had a sickness, but Jesus called her a daughter. What did Jesus previously say about family?

> *"My mother and My brothers are these*
> *who hear the word of God and do it."*
>
> Luke 8:21

The question to be asked is, "Why did Jesus call her a daughter?"

Jesus called the woman "daughter" as an act of compassion, love, and affirmation, recognising her faith despite social insignificance. The term expressed tenderness and included her fully in the spiritual family of Father God, especially since she was an outsider who demonstrated her faith.

The fact she had a blood issue could make all those around her unclean for a short time. We need to note she did two things. First was the reason she touched the "Tzitzit" and secondly, how she was healed. The first could have caused panic amongst the people, but explaining she needed only to touch the "Tzitzit" to be healed, acknowledged Jesus as the Messiah; she was expressing her faith in Jesus as the *"Sun of Righteousness"*.

She only needed to touch this part of the wings to obtain healing. Even though she would need to wait ten days for purification, Jesus said, *"Daughter, be of good cheer; your faith has made you well. Go in peace"* (Luke 8:48). It was not the fact of her touching brought healing, but she believed, exhibited faith, Jesus was the Messiah, the *"Sun of Righteousness"*. Only the *"Sun of Righteousness"* contained healing in the wings of His "Tallit".

Restoration

In the Old Testament, Father God dwelt among the Israelites in the Tabernacle or the Temple, but in the New Testament, Father God dwelt among men in the person of Jesus Christ (John 1:14). Through Jesus, the penalties of the Law are reversed, and the contamination of this world had no effect on Jesus Christ. The woman did not make Jesus (Father God's dwelling) unclean; He made her clean!

Jesus immediately responded to the woman who touched His clothing and was healed. People were pushing and pressing into Him from all over, yet He stopped, turned, and asked, *"Who touched My clothes?"* (Mark 5:30). The disciples were unable to understand what Jesus was saying, but Jesus knew healing power had gone out of Him.

We can't "steal" a miracle from Father God. After the woman came forward and explained herself, Jesus cleared up any misconceptions about her healing, saying, *"Daughter, your faith has made you well. Go in peace, and be healed from your affliction"* (Mark 5:34). Father God is moved to action by our faith, even when He's in the middle of doing something else!

Jesus could have healed the woman and kept on walking to His original destination. Only Jesus and the woman would have known what took place. But He didn't! Jesus stopped what He was doing and acknowledged the result of this woman's faith: her complete and instantaneous healing.

Isn't this a wonderful picture of Salvation, or Restoration? Isn't this what Jesus wants from all of us? To willingly come before Him, bow down, and share with Him our secret desires and concerns, regardless of our circumstances, despite what others might think or say about us?

Overview

"Cleansed and Restored" explores the biblical story of the woman healed by Jesus, her background, and the religious and cultural context.

Summary:

- The woman suffered twelve years of bleeding, was considered unclean, and isolated by Jewish law.
- She touched Jesus's garment, believing in faith she would be healed, referencing the prophecy of healing in the Messiah's "wings" (*Prayer Shawl/Tallit*).
- The act demonstrated deep knowledge of scripture, courage despite risk, and motivated by both physical and emotional suffering.
- Jesus immediately recognised her faith, called her "daughter," and publicly affirmed her wholeness and inclusion in Father God's family.
- The story highlights the significance of faith, the symbolism of the *"Prayer Shawl"*, and Jesus' act of personal restoration, healing both physically and socially.
- Jesus' response showed Father God values faith over law and ritual, and affirms the outcast, restoring them fully.

Prayer Shawl Background:

- The "Tallit", *"Prayer Shawl"*, with tassels (Tzitzit) symbolised obedience and intimacy with Father God; the "wings" connected to healing prophecies.
- Jewish men use the *"Prayer Shawl"* as a personal prayer tent, symbolising refuge and a relationship with Father God.

Restoration:

- The woman's faith resulted in instant healing and public affirmation, showing Salvation and Restoration available through Jesus Christ, not the Law.

Jonah

In the biblical story of Jonah, "Redemption" refers to God's merciful action in rescuing Jonah from his disobedience in the belly of a prepared fish, and also to the Repentance and Salvation of the city of Nineveh, all stemming from God's compassion. Jonah's journey illustrates divine Redemption through a period of suffering and prayer, culminating in his successful, albeit reluctant, mission to Nineveh, which experienced its own Redemption.

When the name Jonah is mentioned, most would think of the "Jonah and the Whale" story, but as we know, Jonah was not swallowed by a whale but a great prepared fish the Lord had made (Jonah 1:17). The question to be asked is, "How and why did Jonah end up in this predicmanent and what was the eventual outcome?"

To answer these questions, we need to first explore:

- Jonah's History
- Jonah's Disobedience
- Jonah's Prayer
- Jonah's Repentance
- Father God's Mercy

Secondly, the outcome of Jonah's obedience:

- Jonah's second chance
- Repentance of Nineveh
- Father God's Mercy
- Father God's Compassion
- Father God works despite us

Jonah's History

The relationship between the children of Israel and the Ninevites was primarily one of conflict and animosity, as Nineveh was a major city of the Assyrian Empire, and the Assyrians were mortal enemies of the Israelites, who were a constant threat and source of suffering for the Israelites.

Jonah was a prophet who lived in the time of Jeroboam 2 (2 Kings 14:25). The pagan Assyrians took many captives and ravaged the countryside. Jonah lived in the village of Gath Hepher, which was 3 miles N/E of Nazareth. He was the only prophet sent to preach to the Gentiles, but as a strong nationalist, was reluctant to go to Ninevah, fully aware of the havoc the Assyrians wrought in Israel over the years.

Jonah's name means "Dove". He was strong-willed, fretful, hasty and faithful to his own, a typical Galilean. Politically, it is obvious he was a loyal lover of Israel and a committed patriot.

While we readily bring to mind the great prepared fish, the Lord prepared five physical things for Jonah:

- A great storm. Jonah 1:4
- A great prepared fish. Jonah 1:17
- A plant. Jonah 4:5
- A worm. Jonah 4:7
- A vehement east wind. Jonah 4:8

As each one brought its own frustration to Jonah, a further question asks, "Why did these come to Jonah?"

Jonah's Disobedience

The story of Jonah highlighted Jonah's relationship with Father God, as the Father's concern is extended to the wicked Ninevites, whom Jonah, a prophet of Israel, despised. The prophet Jonah was tasked by the Lord to deliver a message of warning and repentance to the city of Nineveh, but Jonah hated the Ninevites and, as a result, tried to escape his mission by catching a boat to Tarshish.

Disobedience to the revealed will of Father God is not a good plan to adopt. How much do we go through unnecessarily because we choose to go our own way, do our own thing and not what the Holy Spirit prompts? It should be noted, Tarshish is on the West coast of Spain, some 4000 km West of Joppa. Jonah was told to go East to Nineveh.

Jonah disobeyed Father God, but the Lord gave Jonah an opportunity to ask for forgiveness. Jonah could not possibly foresee what lay ahead because of his disobedience, so the Lord made a final plea to him to rethink. The ship he boarded was a sailing ship, carried cargo and could be rowed. Jonah made his way to the lowest part of the ship and went to sleep. Jonah 1:5

After they set sail, the first act of the Lord was brought into place: a great wind and a mighty tempest. The sails were lowered as the ship began to break up. The cargo on board was thrown into the sea to lighten the ship. While everyone was frantically working to save themselves from disaster, Jonah slept. Jonah 1:5b

The captain of the ship found Jonah and said:

> *"What do you mean sleeper?*
> *Arise, call on your God;*
> *perhaps your God will consider us,*
> *so that we may not perish."*

Jonah 1:6

Many years later, another man by the name of Jesus was sleeping in the stern of their boat, when His disciples woke Him as they were terrified they would perish. A great windstorm had arisen, and the waves were filling the boat with water. Jesus rebuked the wind and said to the sea, *"Peace, be still!"* And the wind ceased, and there was a great calm. Jesus also rebuked the disciples' lack of faith. Mark 4:35–41

Unlike Jesus, Jonah could not speak to the great wind on the sea or the mighty tempest, as he did not have the same relationship with Father God as Jesus did; besides, Jonah was disobedient to the known will of God, whereas Jesus was doing the will of His Father.

The mariners were a mixed bunch who worshipped many gods, as each prayed to his own god (v5). As the violent storm continued, lots were cast to determine who was the cause of this disaster, and Jonah was found guilty. After he was questioned, Jonah replied:

> *"I am a Hebrew;*
> *I fear the Lord,*
> *the God of heaven,*
> *who made the sea and the dry land."*
>
> Jonah 1:9

Jonah had no problem sharing his faith with these heathens, but was not heeding the storm and tempest the Lord had sent to persuade him to repent. How could Jonah pray to a God for deliverance whom he had wilfully disobeyed? The God Jonah knew demanded obedience, although Jonah was aware of the mercifulness of Father God. The men were exceedingly afraid and asked what they should do, to which Jonah replied:

> *"Pick me up and throw me into the sea;*
> *then the sea will become calm for you.*

For I know the great tempest
is because of me."

Jonah 1:12

To these heathen men who worshipped many gods, human sacrifice was acceptable but not preferable. They chose to ignore Jonah's instructions, just as Jonah ignored the Lord's plea to ask for forgiveness and repentance. While the men continued to row harder, the tempest increased until, in desperation, they gave in to Jonah's instructions and prayed to his God:

"We pray, O Lord,
please do not let us perish for this man's life,
and do not charge us with innocent blood;
for You, O Lord,
have done as it pleased You."

Jonah 1:14

Jonah decided to drown rather than go to Nineveh. So, Jonah was thrown into the raging sea, which became calm for the others on board the ship. How often do the actions of others cause havoc to those around us until they are out of the situation?

Everything in this story is miraculous, as the Lord's timing was a miracle. The Lord arranged the ship, used the wind and the waves, and the prepared fish to converge on course at the precise moment and at the exact place. When Jonah was thrown overboard by these sailors, the great prepared fish was there with its mouth open, ready to receive Jonah.

The Bible story mentioned five things Father God prepared for Jonah. As the story is read, a sixth was prepared and set before Jonah. Did Jonah bring to mind the psalm David wrote, where he'd written about Father God supplying our needs?

> *"Thou prepared a table before me*
> *in the presence of my enemies."*

Psalm 23:5

Father God prepares a table for us as we are presented with various situations. While the Father provides for us and blesses us, sometimes the table set before us is not to our liking, but is always for our good to help us grow closer to Him. The table the Lord prepared is tailored to our needs, not our wants, but what is best for us.

Before Jonah was called to take Father God's message to the Ninevehites, the Lord's table was set before him, and travelled with Jonah throughout his journey. As Jonah looked at the prepared table, what were his options? What had Father God provided for him? What was on his table?

As we have free will to choose, discernment is the first thing Jonah should have chosen, followed by obedience; instead, he chose defiance and rebellion. Many items were placed on the table for him, such as prayer, repentance, obedience, understanding, conformity, sorrow, confession, restitution, conviction, restoration, reconciliation, responsibility, regret, resolve, and remorse.

By the end of his journey, other items would replace the previously chosen ones, but only after heartache and stress were taken instead of peace and contentment. Did the Lord prompt Jonah with other words written by David to choose wisely?

> *"Taste and see*
> *that the Lord is good."*
>
> Psalm 34:8

As Jonah chose disobedience instead of conformity and understanding:

> *"The Lord prepared a great fish*
> *to swallow Jonah.*
> *And Jonah was in the belly of the fish*
> *three days and three nights."*
>
> Jonah 1:17

Father God did not create a great fish as His creative acts finished on the sixth day (Genesis 2:1–2), but He prepared a great fish for Jonah. Father God knew the antagonistic heart of Jonah and his reaction to His call would be contrary to the known will of the Father. The Lord had a plan, and the Salvation of the Ninevehites was the outcome. As Jonah chose frustration instead of compliance, Jonah's fate was sealed.

Jonah's Prayer

How long does it take for the penny to drop? Three days! When do you think you would have prayed? When you saw the fish's mouth open? When an hour passed? A day? Are we any different to Jonah? How long do we paddle around in our situations before we call on the Lord and say, "I've had enough, get me out of this?" The Lord does not compel us to go against our will; He just makes us willing to go.

How was Jonah to pray? He was praying to the God he was fleeing from, the Lord who sent the storm so Jonah could cry out, pray for repentance. His disobedience was not the result of thoughtfulness or carelessness, but was planned, calculated, and intentional. Not only did he disagree with the Lord's assignment, but he refused to consider it at all.

Imagine you are inside a prepared fish and unaware when you're going to die. Jonah probably thought being thrown into the sea would be a relatively quick way to drown, although Jonah was obviously conscience through the whole ordeal. Hour after hour, not knowing when his time would arrive to meet the Lord he had denied. No water or food for three days, he cried out to the Lord, but recounts to Him what had happened, as if God didn't already know. Jonah 2:2–9

"You cast me into the sea" (Jonah 2:3). Had Jonah heard what the sailors prayed?

> *"We pray, O Lord,*
> *please do not let us perish for this man's life,*
> *and do not charge us with innocent blood;*
> *for You, O Lord,*
> *have done as it pleased You."*
>
> Jonah 1:14

The fact Jonah called on the Lord in his distress (v2) is proof he belonged to Father God. Although he was a disobedient believer, despite this terrible predicament in which Jonah found himself, he instinctively called out to the Lord.

The general belief, being in the depths of the sea, created a total separation from the Lord, and this is where Jonah found himself as he refers to "Sheol" (Jonah 2:2). Did Jonah imagine he would be separated from Father God? To Jonah's amazement, when he cried out to the Lord from the belly of the prepared fish in the depths of the sea, the Lord heard him instantly. Did Jonah recall the words of Isaiah when he said:

> *"It shall come to pass*
> *that before they call, I will answer;*

and while they are still speaking,

I will hear."

Isaiah 65:24

Understanding came to Jonah as he realised what happened to him was no accident. He was not swept off the deck of the ship by one of the waves, but was *"Cast into the deep"* for the Lord's purpose to be fulfilled. Actions are followed by consequences. The realisation came, he was still required to complete the Lord's will, so he made his prayer:

"When my soul fainted within me,

I remembered the Lord;

And my prayer went up to You,

into Your holy temple.

But I will sacrifice to You

with the voice of thanksgiving;

I will pay what I have vowed.

Salvation is of the Lord."

Jonah 2:7, 9

Jonah understood that praying to idols, other gods, was not the answer, as they could not help in distress or times of trouble. Jonah, previously, could only see through his eyes, where he was to rely on the Lord for his help and protection.

"With the voice of thanksgiving", he would accomplish the task set before him. Despite his agony in the prepared fish, he could sing, for he believed the Lord was dependable and faithful to keep His promises; he knew help was on its way.

Jonah's Repentance

The Lord answered Jonah's prayer as He spoke to the prepared fish, and Jonah was deposited on dry land (2:10). Are we any different? When we are truly sorry for our actions, the Lord hears and answers our prayers. The Lord spoke to the prepared fish, and why not? The Lord prepared the great fish, and He gave it a command the prepared fish clearly understood, and it *"vomited Jonah onto dry land."* Jonah 2:10

But Jonah's ordeal was not over yet, as he may be on dry land and safe, where is he? To get back home again, anywhere on the coast would be approximately 140 km from Gath Hepher, which was near Nazareth. Can you imagine how he must have smelt? Being vomited up, travelling in the hot sun, no change of clothes, remembering he lost all his money and possessions when thrown overboard, as his belongings were left on the ship.

One could only imagine the captain and sailors when Jonah returned to Joppa to claim his possessions left in the mored ship. They had heard the confession of Jonah and experienced the calm after the storm. How this impacted them. Jonah recorded what they did, but what is unclear is whether the sacrifice was on the ship or on land. While *they feared the Lord exceedingly, and offered a sacrifice to the Lord and took vows*, did they believe or add another god to their list of gods? Jonah 1:16

I ask the question, "How did Jonah travel home? Did he walk?" The worst was yet to come as he faced those friends and relatives he left. One could imagine how he bragged to them and was now required to eat humble pie. Shortly, he would tell them he was obeying God's second call to preach to the Ninevites. What do you think his friends and relatives would have said?

Father God's Discipline

Actions always bring consequences, and Jonah's situation was no exception. We need to ask the questions, "Had Jonah really learned his lesson? Had his attitudes changed? Was doing the will of Father God first and foremost in his thinking, or did his bias against the Ninevites get in the way of Father God's plans?"

While we can look back in hindsight and almost judge Jonah for his actions, are we any different? Have we learnt from his past, our past? Do we completely obey Father God's direction no matter what? We are very fortunate to live in the time of grace, but it will not always be like this. I am reminded the scripture says, *"My Spirit will not strive with man forever."* Genesis 6:3

Jonah's Second Chance

"Now the word of the Lord came to Jonah the second time" (Jonah 3:1). Sometimes we just wish the Holy Spirit would leave us alone. We have settled down into our routine and quite content, but the Lord ruffles our pillows and makes us uncomfortable.

We have a choice to either obey or disobey, as life is all about choices. Jonah, on this occasion, chose to obey, so off he went to Nineveh, into the enemy's territory.

Most likely, Jonah preferred the Lord sent someone else to do the job He asked him to do. But Jonah found out he was the Lord's chosen, called for His task. The Lord selected Jonah to do a work nobody else would do as effectively as he could.

Even though Jonah was in enemy territory, the Lord's message was heard and very well accepted. What was Jonah's message? We need to go back to chapter one.

> *"Arise, go to Nineveh, that great city,*
> *and cry out against it;*
> *for their wickedness*
> *has come up before Me."*
>
> Jonah 1:2

Much later, it would be written Jesus said, *"For as Jonah became a sign to the Ninevites"* (Luke 11:30a). The question is, "How did Jonah become a sign to the Ninevites?" The Ninevites had heard what happened to Jonah because of his disobedience before he arrived. They knew all about Jonah, and Father God punished sin. They also learned, the Lord forgives and spares the sinner when they repent.

Repentance of Nineveh

The people of Nineveh did not set their eyes on Jonah. He didn't become a national hero, for the word says, *"So the people of Nineveh believed God"* (Jonah 3:5). This was not about Jonah; he was just the messenger. The response of the people was so spontaneous, they did not wait for orders from the king, but when they heard the Lord's message, they repented.

Jonah was astonished at Father God's dealings with them. Why? Even the King listened to what this foreigner said (Jonah 3:6). You see, the God of the Old Testament was feared. The king decreed the remembrance of God (3:7), made his confession (3:8) and his obedience (3:9). Father God saw their repentance and relented from the disaster He said He would bring upon them, and He did not do it. Jonah 3:10

This was not in Jonah's plan. These people were supposed to be destroyed, as they were the people who brought so much harm to Israel, and Father God spared them! How often do our plans, outcomes, line up with the promptings of the Holy Spirit? Redemption was all about the Lord's will, plan and purpose for the Ninevites.

The Father's will was done (Jonah 3:10). Father God's ultimate plan was for Nineveh to be saved. In the light of this verse, did the Lord change his mind?

> *"For I am the Lord,*
> *I do not change."*
>
> Malachi 3:6

How often, when a situation doesn't turn out the way we expected, do we get angry, have a pity party? You guessed it, this is exactly what Jonah did. The real reason Jonah was disobedient the first time the Lord called is exposed.

> *"Ah, Lord,*
> *was not this what I said when I was still in my country?*
> *Therefore I fled previously to Tarshish;*
> *for I know that You are a gracious and merciful God,*
> *slow to anger and abundant in lovingkindness,*
> *One who relents from doing harm."*
>
> Jonah 4:2

Father God's Mercy

Jonah knew the Lord would save Nineveh if they repented. We can say and do all sought of things and fool those around us, but the Lord looks on the heart and knows our real thoughts, motives and intentions. What didn't Jonah understand about these godless Ninevites in relation to his own disobedience? Was he any better than they were?

The Lord was certainly disappointed with Jonah's attitudes and reactions, but He didn't stop loving him. There was a streak of rebellion in Jonah, which he had to fight. It is possible that Jonah never became a consistently obedient servant of the Lord. He may have been stubborn and prejudiced all his life.

The Lord most likely sent His love and compassion in the form of chastening and discipline. Jonah found out the Lord never leaves His children alone. When we obey Him, He is going to be with us in blessing; when we disobey Him, He is going to be with us in rebuke and chastening. When we are His children, we can't escape Him.

Clearly, Jonah wasn't happy and went and sat in a place east of the city, waiting to see what would happen. It is in these situations, Father God prompts our thoughts with something like, "Why are you angry?" and we are left to work out what we are really doing. God wasn't finished with Jonah; there was still some teaching to do, and Jonah's attitudes needed to change.

Jonah simply begrudged the heathen Ninevites the abundant mercy of Father God. Jonah had gratefully received the Lord's pardoning grace when he repented in the belly of the prepared fish, but was not willing for Nineveh to have the same pardon.

Even when we are in a place we shouldn't be, Father God blesses us. He sent Jonah a plant (4:6) that gave him shade in his stressful state. Jonah thought this was good, but wasn't too pleased when, the next day, a worm Father God had prepared (4:7) killed the tree. Father God then sent a vehement east wind (4:8). Not north, south or west, as this wind was to be annoying.

The sun beat on Jonah, and he grew faint (sunstroke). Father God's question to Jonah is, *"Do you have the right to be angry?"* (4:9). Jonah had pity only for the things that affected him personally (4:10). The Lord's answer to Nineveh was Jonah.

He was the prophet to show right from wrong (4:11). Father God planned Nineveh would be saved, only Jonah's biases got in the way. How better for us to know and choose the Lord's way from the beginning.

Father God's Compassion

The Lord used wonderful logic when dealing with Jonah, as He demonstrated His boundless pity and love to Him as well as to Nineveh. Through the experience of Jonah, we have an amazing account of Father God's mercy and concern for those who are the *"Called"* according to His purpose.

Jonah's experience shows the disappointing picture of how the Lord's own people can be guilty of such gross spiritual negligence or sins of prejudice and rebellion against Father God. We can never escape what the Lord has intended for His own. He will never leave us in our disobedience, because He is our heavenly Father, and we are His children.

Father God Works Despite Us

I find it a shame, the Book of Jonah has often been neglected, as it contains many lessons for each of us. How true is this of our life situations and our dealings with those whom we consider outside of the kingdom? Father God has a plan, and it involves you and me.

The way of holiness is "Complete obedience to the known will of Father God as He reveals Himself to your own heart."

Obedience and the acceptance of it are what Father God requires, nothing less. May we each be aware of the Spirit's leading in our lives, putting our bias aside for Father God and His Kingdom.

Overview

This text explores the biblical story of Jonah, focusing on themes of disobedience, repentance, and Father God's mercy toward both Jonah and Nineveh.

Background

- Jonah was a prophet sent to the enemy city of Nineveh, despite his nationalist feelings and past animosity between Israel and Assyria.
- The Lord prepared five signs for Jonah: a storm, a prepared fish, a plant, a worm, and an east wind.
- Jonah's story is notable for being tasked with ministering to Gentiles.

Disobedience and Consequences

- Jonah disobeyed Father God and tried to flee, causing a miraculous storm at sea.
- His actions brought trouble not only to himself but to others.
- Jonah confessed his fault and was thrown overboard, after which the storm ceased.

Prayer and Repentance

- Inside the prepared fish, Jonah prayed for help and repented after three days, demonstrating both despair and renewed faith.
- Father God answered by having the prepared fish vomit Jonah on dry land.

Second Chance and Nineveh

- Father God gave Jonah a second chance; he preached to Nineveh, and the people, including the king, repented.
- Father God showed mercy and refrained from destroying the city, highlighting divine compassion over human prejudice.
- Jonah was displeased by Father God's mercy but learned about divine compassion and the universality of Father God's grace.

Final Lessons

- Jonah resented Father God's mercy for the Ninevites, revealing his own biases and ongoing struggles with obedience.
- Father God's compassion and persistence with Jonah underscore the broader message: Father God works through flawed people and values obedience.

- Obedience to Father God's will and the dangers of prejudice are central messages.
- The story illustrates Father God cares for all, expects repentance, and can use even reluctant servants for his purposes.

Judah

Judah, the fourth son of Jacob and Leah, was a key figure in biblical history, initially involved in the plot to sell Joseph into slavery but later demonstrating remorse and taking on a leadership role in his family, particularly in the circumstances surrounding his brother Benjamin. Judah's life serves as an example of a flawed but redeemed leader who ultimately submitted to God's will.

As Judah's life is interwoven with his younger brother Joseph, it is helpful to consider the incidents in both brothers' lives before considering Judah's redemption.

Some Situations in Joseph's Life

- Joseph was born to Rachel, Jacob's first love.
- Joseph had ten older brothers and one older sister.
- Joseph was the favoured child.
- Joseph shared his dreams with the family members.
- Joseph informed Jacob about his older brother's misdeeds.
- Joseph, at seventeen, receives a *"Coat of Many Colours"*.
- Joseph was threatened with death but sold to the Ishmaelites.
- Joseph arrived in Egypt.

- Joseph, a slave to Potiphar.
- Joseph falsely accused by Potiphar's wife.
- Joseph imprisoned.
- Joseph interpreted the dreams of the Butler and the Baker.
- Joseph appeared in Pharaoh's court at age thirty.
- Joseph made second in charge to Pharaoh.
- Joseph met his brothers for the first time.
- Joseph met his brothers for the second time.
- Joseph revealed himself to his brothers.

Some Situations in Judah's Life

- Born the fourth son to Leah.
- Conspired with the other brothers to kill Joseph.
- Judah sold Joseph to the Ishmaelites.
- Judah possibly killed a goat, the blood to stain Joseph's coat.
- The coat was sent to Jacob, who presumes Joseph is dead.
- Judah can't deal with remorse and leaves.
- Judah lived in Adullam with Hirah.
- Judah met a Canaanite woman, Shua, and married her.
- Judah had three sons.
- Judah's first son, Er, married Tamar.
- Judah's first wicked son died.
- Judah's second wicked son, Onan, died.
- Judah sent Tamar back to her parents.

- Judah's wife, Shua, died.
- Judah and Hirah go to Timnah for the sheep shearing.
- Judah saw what he thought was a temple prostitute.
- Judah promised a young goat in exchange for her service.
- Judah left his ring, cord, and staff as collateral.
- Judah failed to find the prostitute.
- Judah threatened to burn Tamar for unfaithfulness.
- Judah identified as the father.
- Judah took care of his heirs and returned home to Jacob.
- Judah offered himself as security for the safe return of Benjamin.
- Judah met Joseph in Egypt.

Judah's redemption is a significant biblical story in Genesis where the son of Jacob transitioned from a life of sin and guilt to self-sacrificing love, ultimately becoming the ancestor of the royal line and the Messiah. Initially, Judah was involved in selling his brother Joseph into slavery and later engaged in sinful behaviour.

However, Judah eventually demonstrated a profound change by offering himself as a slave in place of his younger brother Benjamin, demonstrating repentance and a deep understanding of his father's grief. This transformation marks his return to God's favour and explained why his lineage was chosen for the blessing of birthing kings and, eventually, Jesus.

Envy, Jealousy, Malice, Pride

Eleven children were born to Jacob, ten boys and one daughter, from his first wife, Leah, and the two servants Bilhah and Zilpah. Rachel, Jacob's second wife and true love, eventually conceived and gave birth to Jacob's twelfth child, Joseph. Because Joseph was the son of his true love, he was favoured in every way by his father.

The love Jacob constantly showed for Rachel over the other women had not gone unnoticed by their children. By the time Joseph was born, the oldest son, Reuben, would have been about the age of thirteen. One could imagine, at the age of seven, when the eldest was twenty, and most were in their teen years, Joseph would be tagging around behind them, looking for acceptance.

When Joseph reported the wrongdoings of some of his brothers, Jacob saw this behaviour as showing responsibility and presented Joseph with a *"Coat of Many Colours"*. This coat was not an ordinary working coat like all the other brothers would have, as the coat meant leadership in their family. Jacob had, in no uncertain terms, said to the other members in his family, "I am making Joseph the rightful heir to the family inheritance, as he is the first son born to my true love, Rachel!"

Joseph went on to share his dreams about how his family would bow down to him (Genesis 37:7; 9a), firstly to his brothers and sister, then to the complete family. Such dreams brought much antagonism, which only fueled the fire, not smouldering, but burning within each of the older siblings. This was the last nail in Joseph's coffin.

Vengeance

As Jacob knew he could trust Joseph more than the others, he sent him to find his brothers and bring back a report. Joseph set out to find his brothers and the flock of sheep, eventually ending up in a place called Dothan, about eighty miles away from his home. When the other brothers saw Joseph in the distance, they said:

> *"Look, this dreamer is coming!*
> *Come therefore,*
> *let us now kill him and cast him into some pit;*
> *and we will say,*
> *'Some wild beast has devoured him.'*
> *We shall see what will become of his dreams!"*
>
> Genesis 37:19b–20

Reuben, who was the eldest and about thirty years of age, heard what was said, possibly by Simeon and Levi, who had taken revenge for their sister Dinah (Genesis 34:25). The four brothers all had the same mother, Leah, which could have made them around the same age. Reuben 30, Simeon 29, Levi 28, and Judah 27. Reuben did not agree with what was said, but made an alternative suggestion:

> *"Shed no blood, but cast him into the pit*

Judah

> *which is in the wilderness,*
> *and do not lay a hand on him,"*
> *that he might deliver him out of their hands,*
> *and bring him back to his father.*
>
> Genesis 37:22

When the unsuspecting Joseph greeted his brothers, he had no idea what was about to happen.

> *"So it came to pass,*
> *when Joseph had come to his brothers,*
> *that they stripped Joseph of his tunic,*
> *the tunic of many colours that was on him.*
> *Then they cast him into a pit."*
>
> Genesis 37:23–24a

The pleas of Joseph to his brothers went unheeded as he asked for his life to be spared, but the brothers had made up their minds, and there was no turning back. Although they were unanimous in their actions against Joseph, they had no idea the consequences would linger for many years.

While the brothers ate a meal, Joseph was in the pit, and Reuben was away looking after the sheep, a company of Ishmaelites, travelling from Gilead to Egypt, inspired the comment from Judah to his brothers.

> *"What profit is there*
> *if we kill our brother and conceal his blood?*
> *Come and let us sell him to the Ishmaelites,*
> *and let not our hand be upon him,*
> *for he is our brother and our flesh."*
>
> Genesis 37:26–27

Reuben, the eldest, was looking for a way to redeem Joseph from the hands of his evil brothers, while Judah was considering shifting responsibility and making a personal gain from the sale of his stepbrother as a slave. Judah possibly came up with a plan to kill a goat and cover Joseph's coat with the blood, to conceal what he had suggested, but we are not told.

Actions have Consequences

All those present were sworn to secrecy to conceal the truth of what had transpired in Dothan. When the brothers returned home, *they sent the tunic of many colours, and brought it to their father and said, "We have found this. Do you know whether it is your son's tunic or not?"* Jacob recognised the coat and said:

> *"It is my son's tunic.*
> *A wild beast has devoured him.*
> *Without doubt Joseph is torn to pieces."*
>
> Genesis 37:33

So convincing was the evidence, the brothers were not expected to lie or give an explanation, as Jacob had concluded the fate of his favourite son, and thought Joseph had been killed, not thinking there was any other possible answer. Jacob mourned for his son for many days, which would have taken its toll on the other brothers as they knew the truth and the realisation of their actions began to dawn.

When the brothers went to comfort their father Jacob, they were probably not ready for his reply when he said:

> *"For I shall go down into the grave*
>
> *to my son in mourning."*

Genesis 37:35b

As Judah had instigated selling Joseph to the Ishmaelites and profited from his sale, he hadn't expected the depth of devotion and love his father had for this son, who was so despised by the rest of them, except for Benjamin. Judah's life had begun to spiral downward into an unplanned life he had little or no control over, as he would suffer for his actions.

An Unknown Path

Suffering anxiety and remorse, Judah made an excuse to visit a certain Adullamite by the name of Hirah, as he left his home, father, mother and family to cope with the grieving Jacob. Little did he know, his decision would have far-reaching consequences, spanning the best part of twenty years before he returned to his home and family.

One thing to note, Judah and Joseph are now separate from the family. One went willingly, the other did not, but both indicate separation and a turning point for the pair of them. One was a free person to do as he pleased, knowing no bounds; the other was a slave, bound by the rules of others.

As Judah is living with Hirah, he most likely experienced a freedom never before known. He had always respected and obeyed the wishes of his father, Jacob, but this was different, as he made his own way and choices with no one to answer to. We read the following:

> *"And Judah saw there a daughter*
> *of a certain Canaanite whose name was Shua,*
> *and he married her and went into her."*

Genesis 38:2

Judah had no idea what he had unleashed. Maybe he thought he could bring more anguish on Jacob and Leah as he remembered uncle Esau had married a Canaanite woman, which brought bitterness to his father, Isaac and mother Rebekah. He should have recalled his grandmother, Rebekah, instructed his father, Jacob, not to marry a Canaanite woman. Genesis 28:1

We need to understand why Canaanite women were not to be married, as the Canaanites were wicked, and this impacted those who were supposed to be God's chosen people. The Canaanites were descendants of Noah through his son Ham, who had a son whom he called Canaan and were a cursed race because of the sinful actions of Canaan.

As verse two is read and understood, two words stand out, summing up the actions of Judah: "Saw" and "Took". These two words were the preface to others before and after Judah, who, through their actions, spiralled down into further sin.

- Eve "saw" and "took" the forbidden fruit. Genesis 3:6
- The sons of God "saw" and "took" the daughters of men. Genesis 6:2
- Pharaoh's princes "saw" and "took" Abraham's wife. Genesis 12:15
- Shechem "saw" and "took" Dinah, Jacob's daughter. Genesis 34:2
- Achan "saw" and "took" the forbidden spoils. Joshua 7:21
- David "saw" and "took" Bathsheba. 2 Samuel 11:2–4

Only one person "saw" and "took", which enhanced his relationship with Father God. Abraham was instructed by Father God to sacrifice his son, Isaac, which, although Abraham did not understand, he obediently complied with the known will of the Father. Genesis 22:3

Such was the faith of Abraham, his words to the two men who were with them projected his trust in Father God when he said:

> *"Stay here with the donkey;*
> *the lad and I will go yonder and worship,*
> *and we will come back to you."*
>
> Genesis 22:5

Abraham "saw" and "took" Isaac, the wood, the knife and fire, but no lamb for the sacrifice. When Abraham was questioned by his son, his reply was:

> *"My son,*
> *God will provide for Himself*
> *the lamb for a burnt offering."*
>
> Genesis 22:8a

Abraham "saw" and "took" Father God at His promised word. When they arrived at the appointed place, *Abraham built an altar there and placed the wood in order; and he bound Isaac his son and laid him on the altar, upon the wood. And Abraham stretched out his hand and took the knife to slay his son.* Abraham "saw" and "took" the knife.

The Angel of the Lord called to Abraham and told him not to harm his son, because of his obedience to Father God's command. Then Abraham lifted his eyes and looked, and there behind him was a ram caught in a thicket by its horns.

"So Abraham went and took the ram,
and offered it up for a burnt offering
instead of his son."

Genesis 22:13b

Abraham "saw" and "took" the ram, which he offered as a sacrifice to the Father, which brought glory to Father God. Only what Abraham "saw" and "took" continued to bring glory to Father God, where all the others brought glory to man.

Many years would pass before the New Testament writer, John, the cousin of Jesus, would write in his first epistle exactly what the "saw" and "took" represented when he wrote:

"Do not love the world or the things of the world.
If anyone loves the world,
the love of the Father is not in Him.
For all that is in the world,
the lust of the flesh,
the lust of the eyes,
and the pride of life
is not of the Father but is the world.

1 John 2:15–16

Father God's Plan

Judah entered a twenty-year plan, as his attitudes and outlook on life would change, as pain and suffering continued to be his companions, until the Lord saw fit to bring Judah to his knees in repentance. His life dealt with joy, disharmony, sorrow, grief, and death. Such was the road Judah chose to walk.

Judah and his wife Shua eventually had two sons, followed later by a third. The first was called Er, the second Onan and the third Shelah, but the two older sons grew up to be wicked, which indicated what happened behind the scenes in Jacob's home.

Judah "saw" and "took" a wife for Er, by the name of Tamar (Genesis 38:6), who was a Canaanite. Although we are not told, one could imagine that both Er and Tamar were wild children, juveniles, complementing each other in everything they did. Tradgety came upon this couple when Er died because of his wickedness, which left Tamar childless and a widow.

Judah instructed his next son, Onan, to marry Tamar, so his deceased brother would have an heir for his inheritance. One could imagine Onan was an adolescent, and while the idea of being intermate with Tamar appealed to him, responsibility for a family was way out of his thinking. Because his actions displeased Father God, he suffered the same fate as his older brother and died.

Two young teenage boys had died, which left Judah with his third child, Shelah, who was too young to be married, so he told Tamar to return to her family and wait, which meant Tamar was to live as a widow until the next son, Shelah, was of an age to marry and give her children.

Judah's decision and lifestyle hadn't escaped the eyes of Father God, as He intentionally broke oral laws accepted by those who were descendants of Abraham. Judah was once again devastated when his wife Shua died, leaving him with a grown son, Shelah and a daughter-in-law, Tamar.

After a suitable time of mourning, Judah, along with his friend Hirah, went to Timnah, where Judah would oversee the shearing of his sheep completed by the other shepherds. While the sheep would be shorn, revelry with the other shepherds would be the focus. As the two men walked the road, suddenly and unexpectedly, Judah noticed a woman sitting in an open place and presumed she was a temple prostitute.

With the full knowledge of his friend Hirah, Judah made a deal with the woman and promised her a young goat for her services. While the woman agreed, she asked for a pledge of his ring, cord and staff. Although Judah may have thought the request or pledge obscure, he obliged and presented the items to her safekeeping until the young goat was sent.

Judah and his brothers previously killed a young goat to stain the coat of Joseph to decieve Jacob into thinking Joseph was dead. Presenting a young goat to this woman was a deception to cover up his sins. When Judah and Hirah returned home:

> *"Judah sent the young goat*
> *by the hand of his friend the Adullamite,*
> *to receive his pledge*
> *from the woman's hand,*
> *but he did not find her."*
>
> Genesis 38:20

Hirah made inquiries about the woman, but everyone denied such a woman existed. When he returned to Judah and told him what had happened, Judah said:

> *"Let her take them for herself,*
> *lest we be shamed;*
> *for I sent this young goat*
> *and you have not found her."*
>
> Genesis 38:23

Time hastened on, and Judah was told his daughter-in-law was pregnant by harlotry. He was very quick to judge Tamar for her actions and decreed she should be publicly burned. For Judah, this could be the answer to avoid giving his other son to this woman. Had he regretted his decision to wed Er and Tamar? But Father God is not done with Judah by any stretch of the imagination, as all is about to be revealed.

Revealed

When Tamar was brought out to face the judgment for her deeds, she revealed to those who gathered to watch the spectacle, pointed out who the father of her child was as she produced a ring, a cord and a staff, and then asked the owner to identify himself. Judah hadn't expected this turn of events and humbly acknowledged they belonged to him. By his own actions, he shamed himself and admitted his multiple sins.

Judah confessed this Canaanite woman, Tamar, was more righteous than himself. What Judah was saying, a righteous person not only does the right thing for other people, but follows the laws of their religion. An embarrassed, broken man, Judah accepted the responsibility for Tamar and her child, as he would take care of them all as was the custom of his culture.

Pride came before a fall; surely this was the case for Judah. Disgraced in the Canaanite community, Judah returned to his home with Jacob and his family. So much had happened in the past twenty years, Judah was not the person who left, as he returned humbled, disgraced, widowed, a son, Shelah, a daughter-in-law, Tamar, and twin sons, Perez and Zerah.

Notice all the deception. People lie, deceive, and act immorally. Judah was responsible for providing a husband for Tamar, which is highlighted by the fact she is called his "daughter-in-law" (v16). Judah broke his promise to Tamar, and Tamar, to secure her position and inheritance through Judah, deceived him as a result.

Broken promises and lies drove everything in the lives of all involved. Yet in all of this, Father God was faithful and had a plan, though the people involved were wicked. Father God can and will use terribly flawed people to bring about greater purposes.

So what was the thread that ran through this whole ordeal? The promised seed, the bloodline, was to pass through Judah. His wife and two sons were eliminated, and Tamar, a substitute, brought forth the son who would carry the bloodline through to Jesus Christ.

Back Home with Jacob

A drought has seized the land, and as none of the brothers had any survival skills, Jacob suggested, *"Indeed I have heard that there is grain in Egypt; go down to that place and buy for us there, that we may live and not die." So Joseph's ten brothers went down to buy grain in Egypt.* Genesis 42:2–3

Judah had returned home to Jacob and faced the prospect of travelling with his nine brothers to secure grain. None of them could imagine what lay ahead in the coming days, would shake them to the very core of their being. How the skeletons in their past would test them to the point of breaking, because of the plan Father God had in place for His promises made previously to Abram.

When the ten brothers arrived in Egypt, their objective was to buy grain and leave. Were they ready for the unexpected? The Overseer questioned them as to their real purpose and accused them of being spies. Unable to absolve themselves, the Overseer imprisoned them all together, to test them about the truth contained in what they told him about their home and family.

Three days would pass before the Overseer came to see them with an alternative plan for them to follow. They could leave, except one would remain in prison until they returned. Their return was dependent on the younger brother attending with them. What choice did they have but to obey the commands given to them?

Reuben, the eldest, remembered the act they committed in the past as Father God's retribution was on them all (Genesis 42:22). While they spoke together in their own language, it appeared that the Overseer was aware and understood everything they said. Simeon was taken before their eyes, bound and led away to wait their return.

But the worst was yet to be, which would add more drama to their present journey. The money used to pay for their grain was in the top of each man's sack. They had professed to be honest men! How could they return and justify the money in their sacks, and as an extra, their youngest brother, Benjamin, was required to return with them? What had they done?

When the nine brothers returned home without Simeon, Jacob was not happy. A simple journey to obtain grain to sustain their family had blown out into an apparent disaster, as Jacob said:

> *"You have bereaved me:*
> *Joseph is no more,*
> *Simeon is no more,*
> *and you want to take Benjamin.*
> *All these things are against me.*
> *My son shall not go down with you."*

Genesis 42:36, 38b

Judah was part of all that happened, plus he had other issues to deal with. He not only had an extended family, but also those in his own care to think about. The grain soon ran out, and it is now Judah who takes the spotlight and approached his father with his plan to hopefully convince Jacob to agree with him. After reminding his father of the conditions set by the Overseer, Judah said:

> *"Send the lad with me,*
> *and we will arise and go,*
> *that we may live and not die,*
> *both we and you and also*
> *our little ones."*

Genesis 43:8

Jacob saw the change evident in Judah as he listened to what he said and agreed. When Judah included *"our little ones"*, was he referring to his own children Perez and Zerah? Jacob gave some more suggestions by taking double money and some gifts that would prove they were who they said they were and from where they lived. It would be an emotional scene as Jacob bid farewell to his most precious son, Benjamin.

Ten different brothers made their way back to Egypt, as their mixed emotions brought some anxiety; they had no idea what their fate would be this time. Something so routine for most proved to be a disaster for them. Soon they would stand before the Overseer again, asking to buy more grain. They had completed all he asked, but would it be enough?

As the brothers stood in line, they were suddenly ushered away to the Overseer's home and were told to wait, as he would be dining with them at noon. When they arrived, the brothers talked to the steward, who assured them all was in order. They were given water to wash their feet and feed for their donkeys. This was nothing like they expected. What ulterior motive did this Overseer have?

Simeon was reunited with his brothers as they sat together. When the Overseer came into his home, all the brothers bowed before him to the earth (Genesis 43:26). He asked them many questions about their family and father. Again, they prostrated themselves before him (v28). When he inquired about the youngest son, he made a hasty retreat from the room, but when he returned, the Overseer served each person with their meal.

Early the following morning, at dawn, the brothers left to make their way back to their father Jacob. They were relieved all had gone so well, though not at all what they expected. The brothers noticed the steward from the Overseer's home approached them in haste. What could he possibly want?

The steward explained, the Overseer's silver cup was missing, and he was sent to search their belongings. The person who had the cup would be his lord's slave. While the brothers proclaimed their innocence, the search revealed the missing cup in Benjamin's sack, so they all returned to the home of the Overseer, where he waited patiently for them.

The overseer spoke harshly to them as they fell to the ground before him (Genesis 44:14). Judah, not Reuben, responded to the Overseer:

"What shall we say to my lord?

What shall we speak?

Or how shall we clear ourselves?

God has found out the iniquity of your servants;

here we are, my lord's slaves,

both we and he also

with whom the cup was found."

Genesis 44:16

The Overseer made no apology for what would happen. The nine brothers were free to leave, but Benjamin would remain and become his slave. Judah then reapproached the Overseer and explained how he took responsibility for Benjamin to return him safely to his father. If this were not done, the father would surely grieve and die. Judah then provided a substitute in himself when he said:

> *"Now therefore, please let your servant remain*
> *instead of the lad as a slave to my lord,*
> *and let the lad go up with his brothers.*
> *For how shall I go up to my father*
> *if the lad is not with me,*
> *lest perhaps I see the evil*
> *that would come upon my father."*
>
> Genesis 44:33–34

The brothers were not expecting what would happen next, as this was not in their expectations at all. Suddenly and without warning, the Overseer told everyone to leave his presence, but the brothers were to stay. Everyone obeyed the orders of the Overseer. As the brothers watched, the Overseer, instead of wreaking more carnage on them, began to cry profusely. When the Overseer composed himself, he said to the brothers in their language:

"Please come near to me."
So they came near.
Then he said,
"I am Joseph your brother,
whom you sold into Egypt."

Genesis 45:4

As Joseph was thirty-nine years old, twenty-two years had passed since his brothers sold him to the Ishmaelites. As Joseph explained there was still another five years of famine, they were to return home and bring Jacob, all their families and belongings and live in Goshen, a suburb of Egypt, where they would be looked after.

One could only imagine the conversation the brothers would need to have with their father, Jacob, about their past transgressions. Judah was the real spokesman, not Ruben, the only one willing to take responsibility for the hard situations. Flawed, yes, but a man who was willing to admit his wrongs and try to make amends.

Jacob would listen to Judah, maybe with some anger as everything unfolded, how they had no concern for the grief he had and held, as Jacob's response was:

Judah

> *"It is enough.*
> *Joseph my son is still alive.*
> *I will go and see him before I die."*
>
> Genesis 45:28

Judah was the one who led the way to reunite Joseph with Jacob, as Judah became a leader in the family, the one through whom they could find their path to reconciliation (Genesis 46:28). Judah, the fourth son of Leah, had proven himself to be the true leader of their family. The tribe of Judah would eventually form the bloodline to the foretold Messiah.

Jacob's blessing would remain on Judah, for his final words were:

> *"Judah, you are he whom your brothers shall praise;*
> *Your hand shall be on the neck of your enemies;*
> *Your father's children shall bow down before you."*

> *"The sceptre shall not depart from Judah,*
> *nor a lawgiver from between his feet,*
> *until Shiloh comes;*
> *and to Him shall be the obedience of the people."*
>
> Genesis 49:8, 10

Overview

Joseph:

- Joseph was Jacob's favoured son, leading to jealousy and betrayal by his brothers.
- Joseph's reporting of dreams and wrongdoings intensified his brothers' animosity, culminating in his being sold into slavery by Judah's suggestion.
- Joseph endured slavery, false accusations, imprisonment and eventually rose to second-in-command in Egypt.

Judah:

- Judah took a leadership role but acted out of jealousy and deceit, selling Joseph and covering it up.
- Struggled with guilt, left his family for years, married a Canaanite woman, and experienced family tragedies.
- Deceived by Tamar, leading to personal humiliation but eventual acceptance of responsibility.
- Judah returned humbled, became a spokesperson for his brothers, and offered himself as a substitute for Benjamin.

Themes and Outcomes:

- Recurrent themes of envy, betrayal, suffering, and eventual repentance.
- Father God's plan unfolds despite human flaws, using Judah's lineage for the future royal and Messianic line.
- Judah's transformation from a flawed perpetrator to a self-sacrificing leader ensured his family's survival and fulfilment of Father God's promises.

Tamar

Tamar's story in the Bible (Genesis 38) is a tale of betrayal, desperation, and divine providence, where Father God orchestrated a scandal into a powerful act of Redemption by including her in the lineage of Jesus Christ. Her life can be divided into the following sections, which reveal much about Tamar and her life's path, chosen by Father God.

- Tamar's Story
- Promises made
- Promises broken
- Plan of Action
- Security
- More Righteous
- Outcome

Tamar's Story

Judah was the fourth son of Jacob, who left home and family to live in Chezib, where he met and married a Canaanite woman by the name of Shua, who bore him three children, Er, Onan and Shelah. In the passage of time:

Tamar

> *"Judah took a wife for Er his firstborn,*
> *and her name was Tamar.*
> *But Er was wicked in the sight of the Lord,*
> *and the Lord killed him."*
>
> Genesis 38:6–7

Tamar married Judah's eldest son, Er, but because he was wicked in the Lord's eyes, he died. While the Bible does not explain in detail the wickedness of Er, the consensus was he worshipped idols, had no interest in Father God's law and exploited others. Wicked men didn't usually make good husbands, so we can assume their marriage was fraught with problems for Tamar.

The marriage to Er had produced no children, so Judah instructed the second son to supply an heir for the deceased, which in the future was known as a "Levirate Marriage". A widow would marry a brother-in-law, and the first son produced was considered the legal descendant of her dead husband. Judah told Onan:

> *"Go into your brother's wife and marry her,*
> *and raise up an heir to your brother."*
>
> Genesis 38:8

Onan was more than willing to sleep with Tamar, but, unfortunately, he did not desire to have a child with her. He was aware the major part of the inheritance went to him. Onan was taking selfish advantage of the widow, as he was content to be intimate with his sister-in-law, but purposefully avoided impregnating her. Father God called Onan's actions "wicked" and killed him. Genesis 38:10

Promises Made

The only son left was Shelah, who was much younger than his brothers, so Judah promised Shelah would marry Tamar in due course, but it was clear she became a burden to his family. Judah was concerned, afraid Tamar might bring about the death of his youngest son, and so was more interested in protecting him than obligations to a daughter-in-law.

Judah's answer was to send Tamar back to her father to live as a childless widow with the promise of marriage in the future, when Shelah was old enough. The stigma attached to Tamar in this situation would be overwhelming, as she likely had no money or other options. She would not have any priority within her birth family and was promised in marriage, which meant she was not allowed to marry outside her husband's family.

Promises Broken

A broken promise refers to a commitment not fulfilled, as it implies a failure to uphold a stated agreement, leading to feelings of disappointment, betrayal, and damage to trust. The Bible generally views broken promises negatively, as a violation of trust and a failure to live up to one's word, emphasising lack of integrity and faithfulness on behalf of the promise giver.

The Bible also presents Father God as faithful and reliable, never breaking His promises and promotes truthful and reliable communication, with Jesus stating:

> *"But let your 'Yes' be 'Yes,'*
> *and your 'No,' 'No.'*
> *For whatever is more than these*
> *is from the evil one."*

Matthew 5:37

The Bible consistently portrays Father God as perfectly faithful:

> *"God is not a man,*
> *that He should lie,*
> *nor a son of man,*
> *that He should repent."*

Numbers 23:19a

Father God does not change His mind (Malachi 3:6), as believers are called to emulate Father God's faithfulness by being reliable and trustworthy in their commitments. The Bible acknowledges human failure and the need for Father God's help to keep commitments, recognising people struggle to live up to their promises.

As Tamar was very aware her childbearing days were limited, Shelah was fully grown and had not been offered to her in marriage, she accepted the fact she was never going to be Shelah's wife, and her options for childbearing were diminishing. After twice widowed and denied her rightful inheritance by her father-in-law, Judah, Tamar devised a plan to secure justice.

Plan of Action

News came that Tamar's mother-in-law died, and Judah was mourning for his wife (v12). At the end of his public grief, Judah, along with his friend Hirah, was leaving to join the men shearing his sheep in a place called Timnah, close enough for Tamar to go and meet him.

As Judah and Hirah were travelling with the expressed purpose to join the shearers, which meant they would oversee the shearers' work, then share with the shearers in revelry and drunkenness. Had the covenant Father God put in place with the children of Israel meant anything to this man?

Father God's covenant with Israel was the Mosaic Covenant, established at Mount Sinai. The Israelites covenanted to obedience, including the Ten Commandments. Father God's favour was conditional on their compliance, as He would bless those who followed His commands faithfully, while disobedience would lead to punishment.

For Tamar to meet Judah in her widow's clothes was not appropriate, so she disguised herself, put on a veil, and sat in an open space on the road they would take, outside the entrance to Enaim. When Judah saw her, he assumed she was a temple prostitute, approached her and asked if he could come in to her. As the woman consented, Judah fixed a price of a young goat.

The woman asked for some promissory items until the young goat arrived. This was nothing out of the ordinary, but while it may have seemed odd to Judah, she wanted his ring, cord and staff; whatever he thought, he complied. Satisfied with himself, the two proceeded to their destination for revelry with the shearers.

The question to be asked is, "What is the meaning behind the ring, cord and staff?" The ring represents identity and status, the cord signifies his personal status as a leader, and the staff is a mark of his authority as a prominent individual. For a deeper understanding of what each item contained, the following explanation is given.

- **Ring.** The ring was an ancient equivalent of a signet ring, used to leave a unique impression on documents or objects and served as a signature, a stamp of identity, and a symbol of authority and truth.
- **Cord.** The cord refers to the fringes on the hem of Judah's garment, maybe his prayer shawl. It was a bond of connection, and in a spiritual context, relates to fulfilling the law of God or even a divine covenant.
- **Staff.** The staff was a walking stick or a symbol of identification for a leader, which represented authority and power, and giving it away was a significant gesture of relinquishing one's position.

The ring, cord, and staff represent the emblems of the individual's personal status, much like an ancient identity card. The fact Judah possessed a ring, wore a garment decorated with tassels, or wore his ring with a cord as jewellery, carried a staff in his hand attests to his high status and importance as a leader.

Security

Tamah, satisfied she had received justice, waited for the outcome as she removed the disguise and replaced it with her garments of widowhood. Three months later, Tamar found she was with child. Rumours spread about Tamar's pregnancy, and Judah was quick to take action as he ordered her to be burned to death for prostitution.

Tamar confessed to the identity of the father by producing the ring, cord and staff. Judah's actions now exposed, confessed that Tamar was more righteous because he did not give her Shelah as a husband. Eventually, although Judah never took her to wife, Tamar produced twins.

As Tamar gave birth, the midwife tied a scarlet thread around the hand that came out of the womb first, but then withdrew, allowing the second twin to be born first. The firstborn was called "Perez", and the second "Zerah".

More Righteous

When Judah recognised his possessions, he acknowledged his own unrighteousness and confessed Tamar was more righteous than himself because he had denied her the right to marry Shelah. Judah's statement was a full admission of his guilt for his part in the deceit and failure to follow through with his legal obligations to his son's widow.

Being righteous literally means to be right, especially in a moral way. Those who hold religious views often talk about being righteous, which means the person not only does the right thing for other people but also follows the laws of their religion.

Integrity and blamelessness are two characteristics that partner with righteousness, often describing people as free from guilt or sin and are characterised by their integrity and soundness of character. They treat others with the respect and dignity they deserve.

Behaviour portrays the inner person, as they are careful when choosing the company or friends they associate with, avoiding people who engage in wicked or sinful deeds. Judah failed in all ways, disgracing himself, a respected leader in the community in which he lived.

Outcome

Tamar's story challenges us not to judge people for actions they take out of desperation, as people often focus on Tamar's wrongdoing, including deception and prostitution. Yet in the passage, it is the disobedient men who are judged. Er died because he was wicked. Onan was judged because he failed to honour his brother's widow. Judah was judged because he had wronged Tamar, but confessed his sin and repented, saying she is more righteous.

As Judah acknowledged his wrongdoing and sinfulness, Tamar's lineage became the path for the birth of Perez, and subsequently, King David and Jesus, illustrating how Father God used even the most unlikely individuals to fulfil His redemptive purposes.

Overview

Tamar's story in Genesis 38 is about broken promises, bold actions, and eventual justice, showing how Father God used surprising people in His larger plan.

Main Incidents

- Tamar marries Er, Judah's son, but Er died due to wickedness.
- Judah asks his second son, Onan, to give Tamar a child (Levirate marriage), but Onan refused and died for his disobedience.
- Judah promised his youngest son, Shelah, to Tamar, but delayed and never fulfilled this promise, leaving Tamar widowed and childless.

Tamar's Plan

- Realising Judah will not keep his promise, Tamar disguised herself as a prostitute and had relations with Judah, obtaining his ring, cord, and staff as collateral.

Consequences

- Tamar became pregnant with twins. Perez and Zerah
- When accused of immorality, she revealed Judah was the father by producing his personal items.
- Judah admitted his fault and declared her "more righteous" than he is, as he failed in his responsibilities.

Significance

- Tamar's actions secured her place in the family and the lineage of King David and Jesus.
- Tamar's story highlights Father God's faithfulness and ability to redeem difficult situations.

Rahab

A Story of Faith, Courage and Redemption

In the grand narrative of the Bible, few stories are as compelling as Rahab, a woman of Jericho whose faith and courage changed the course of history. Though often remembered as "Rahab the prostitute", her past did not define her future. Hebrews 11:31

Rahab's choice to trust in the God of Israel made her a hero of faith and a direct ancestor of Jesus Christ, as her story is one of redemption, bravery, and the incredible power of choosing Father God over fear.

Who was Rahab?

Rahab lived in Jericho, a city destined for destruction as the Israelites moved to claim the land Father God promised Abram. Rahab was not a lady of the night, but the temple high priestess in Baal worship. She represented Asherah, Baal's consort. The people were taught, when Baal and Asherah were intimate, the outcome was fertility for their land.

As the priests and consorts imitated the gods and consented to sexual love, the land was thought to be fertilised. This was Rahab, and as she also owned an establishment for travellers to stay in, it was the ideal place to socialise. Because she was a high priestess, Rahab was held in high regard; her word would not be doubted or questioned.

However, Rahab was also a woman of great intelligence and discernment, as her actions demonstrated an understanding of Father God's power, which many Israelites lacked.

Rahab's Journey Begins

As Joshua was the leader of the Israelites, he chose two men to leave Acacia Grove and secretly spy out the land, especially Jericho. The two spies were faithful in what Joshua asked them to accomplish, and stayed in the house of a harlot named Rahab. As they mingled with the guests, the two spies gleaned much information about the land from the travellers who lodged there.

The two spies hadn't blended in, as the king of Jericho was told of their presence, so he sent word to Rahab:

> *"Bring out the men who have come to you,*
> *who have entered your house,*
> *for they have come to search out all the country."*
>
> Joshua 2:3

When Rahab received the message from the king, it confirmed her thoughts, and she took evasive action. The Lord had brought the two spies under the protection of the one person in all Jericho who believed in Him. Rahab understood and recognised why they were there, so she ignored the king's messengers and provided protection by hiding them on her roof.

Rahab misled the king by providing false information about the Israelites' whereabouts, and because she was held in high regard, she was believed. No one would doubt the word of the high priestess of Baal. Rahab was a respected woman, as her actions demonstrated an understanding of Father God's power.

Rahab's Confession

The journey of the children of Israel was monitored for a long time, and their conquests by the inhabitants of Jericho. Over the many years since the plagues the Egyptians contended with, the victories over the Egyptians were well documented by those in the land of Canaan.

Rahab was well aware of the Israelites' history, even though their travels had spanned over forty years since leaving Egypt. As a young girl, one could imagine the talk around the family table at meal times and the prospect of an invasion. A huge sigh of relief was experienced when all went quiet for forty years, as the Israelites wandered aimlessly in the desert.

Rahab listened to what was shared by her parents and processed each event. Was Father God preparing her for the future throughout all the years, for the present time she found herself confronted with? Rahab recognised the Israelites possessed a Godly protection sadly lacking throughout the land and people where she lived.

As the city gates were closed and the situation appeared to be calm, Rahab met with the two spies and revealed what she had gleaned from all she had heard and processed.

"I know that the Lord has given you the land.
For we have heard how the Lord dried up
the water of the Red Sea for you
when you came out of Egypt,
and what you did to the two kings of the Amorites
whom you utterly destroyed.

As soon as we heard these things,
our hearts melted;
neither did there remain any more courage
in onyone because of you,

for the Lord your God,
He is God in heaven above
and earth beneath."

Joshua 2:9–11

Protection

The Lord God brought the two spies under the protection of the one person in all Jericho who believed in Him. But Rahab had a plan to save not only herself but her family as well. Rahab covenanted with the two spies because she rescued them from certain peril and possible death. In return, she asked for her and her family's lives to be spared. Joshua 2:12–14

When evasive action was taken by the king, the gates shut, a covenant was made and agreed to with the two spies to preserve Rahab and her family's lives, as she let them down through the window in the side of the wall where her home was situated. The spies told her:

> *"When we come into the land,*
> *you bind this line of scarlet cord in the window*
> *through which you let us down,*
> *bring your father, your mother, your brothers,*
> *and all your fathers's household*
> *to your own home."*
> *Then she said,*
> *"According to your words,*
> *so be it."*

Joshua 2:18, v21

Three Days

Among some of the many incidents associated with this story are the instructions Rahab gave to the two spies as she was about to let them down by a rope through her window.

> *"Get to the mountain,*
> *lest the persuers meet you.*
> *Hide there three days,*
> *until the persurers have returned.*
> *Afterward you may go your way."*
>
> Joshua 2:16

This was another window of safety the two spies were called to observe. Three days in the Bible often symbolised divine intervention, new life, and a prophetic timeline pointing to Jesus' resurrection. Jesus referred to His being in the grave, similar to Jonah in the belly of the prepared fish. Saul was blind for three days before enlightenment came.

Many occurrences in the Old Testament serve as types of the ultimate act of Resurrection and Salvation, others bring knowledge, while security is always a keen side track, sometimes necessary to walk for your physical safety and more often spiritual enlightenment. At other times, Father God says, "Wait", or "Pause a moment. I've got this."

The Scarlet Cord

When the spies told Rahab to tie the scarlet cord in the window, they possibly reflected on the time when their ancestors had left Egypt and were instructed to place blood on the doorposts and lintel for protection, avoiding disaster. A scarlet cord would be representative of the blood and protected Rahab and her family as long as they stayed inside the home.

Rahab understood and recognised why the spies were there. She had deceived the king's messengers to provide protection by hiding them on her roof, then letting them down through the window in the side of the wall where her home was situated.

Rules governed Rahab and her family, who were sworn to secrecy. Not carrying out what was agreed to would dissolve the covenant, and the two spies would be blameless. Rehab demonstrated trust in the spies by carrying out their instructions, by tying the scarlet cord in her window for them to recognise when the assault was over.

The two spies knew victory was assured because Rahab had aided them in their effort to gather information for Joshua, as their confession was:

> *"Truly the Lord has delivered*
> *all the land into our hands,*
> *for indeed all the inhabitants of the country*
> *are fainthearted because of us."*

Joshua 2:24

To understand what was arranged by the two spies, you need to explore the Hebrew word used for *cord*, which is "Tikvah" (Joshua 2:18). "Tikvah" means *hope, expectation,* or a *cord/rope,* meaning "to gather together, wait for, bind, or hope for." A firm, optimistic belief in a better future, rather than just a fleeting desire.

The concept is beautifully illustrated when Rahab ties a scarlet cord (Tikvah) in her window as a guarantee of safety for her family, symbolising a literal binding to a promise and a symbolic hope for the future. The cord serves as a tangible representation of hope, a lifeline to cling to during difficult times. Hope is often intertwined with faith, as faith provides the assurance of those hoped-for promises.

Hope Anticipated

As Rahab watched each day as the children of Israel marched around the city and then returned to camp, one could imagine what she and her family were thinking. *What were they waiting for? Why don't they attack? Are they afraid?* Each family member huddled together in Rahab's home.

The seventh day was different as the Israelites continued to march around and around the city, seven times. The guards on the walls were probably complacent as nothing had happened previously, but then, like a flash of lightning, in the twinkling of an eye, as a thief in the night, the trumpets sounded, the people shouted out with a loud voice, and the front wall of the fortified city of Jericho fell down flat. Joshua 6:20

Joshua saw the two messengers who made the covenant with Rahab and told them to rescue her household and their possessions. As the two messengers looked at the remaining walls, the scarlet cord could be seen, in place as Rahab had been instructed to do, so they knew exactly where to go and rescue her and her household.

Mass destruction was on every hand as the inhabitants were put to the sword. Presently, there was a knock on the door of Rahab's home. Was it their neighbours, or the soldiers, who were seeking to enter? As Rahab hesitantly opened the door, there stood the two spies whom she protected all those weeks ago. True to the covenant made, Rahab and her family were saved from this terrible calamity.

The two messengers found Rahab along with the other members of her family and took them to a safe place outside the camp of Israel. The scene was horrific as they witnessed everyone killed and all the treasure brought out and placed in the treasury, which belonged to the Lord, then Jericho was set ablaze. The children of Israel understood the city was declared as belonging to the Lord because He had said:

> *"Now the city shall be doomed by the Lord*
> *to destruction, it and all who are in it.*
> *Only Rahab the harlot shall live,*
> *she and all who are with her in the house,*
> *because she hid the messengers that were sent."*

Joshua 6:17

The faith of Rahab saved herself and those near and dear to her from utter destruction. It was an uneasy feeling for the high priestess of Baal to be among those who believed in the One True God. How would they react to them as they joined the camp? What would become of them now? Was it worth them betraying all their friends? As they watched, Joshua placed a curse on their beloved city, which now lay in ruins. Joshua 6:26

Hope Realised

Joshua took these refugees and placed them in the care of those in the tribe of Judah, where they'd be instructed in the ways of the Israelites. Rahab and her family embraced the Israelites' ways because they were grateful for how they'd been saved and given a new life, as they didn't grumble or complain like some of the other Israelites.

Rahab had no idea when she protected the two messengers, because she feared the God of the Israelites more than their own gods, she was inducted into the plan of Redemption, and would help to fulfil the third blessing given to Abram, that the Israelites would be a blessing to others. Genesis 12:1–3

Acceptance

Rahab was about to experience a situation that would completely change her and her family's beliefs forever, if they were to remain in the *"Covenant community"*. In time, Rahab fell in love with a Judean by the name of Salmon. So what were the consequences associated with this act of sincere love to an Israelite of the tribe of Judah?

"An Ammonite or Moabite
shall not enter the assembly of the Lord;
even to the tenth generation
none of his descendants
shall enter the assembly of the Lord forever."

Deuteronomy 23:3

This Old Testament Law, or Mosaic Law, was meant to protect Israel from pagan influence, so how could Rahab marry Salmon and be accepted? Father God viewed such violations could impact the community for a significant period, ten generations or forever.

The restrictions on who may enter the assembly emphasised the holiness required of those who came before the Lord. This reflected the broader biblical theme of holiness, where Father God's people are called to be set apart and pure, both individually and collectively. The assembly is a place where Father God's presence is acknowledged, and His standards are upheld.

The Assembly of the Lord was not just a social or political group, but a religious one that expressed and maintained the covenant relationship with Father God. Entrance into this assembly often required a certain level of holiness and purity, reflecting the presence of Father God in their midst.

Rahab had made her confession known to the two spies when she talked with them.

"For the Lord your God,
He is God in heaven above
and earth beneath."

Joshua 2:11

Rahab had acknowledged and accepted the first commandment set down by Father God:

"You shall have no other gods
before Me."

Exodus 20:3

As Joshua was the leader of the children of Israel, he would have dealt with this situation. First was the covenant his two trusted men made with her; now, Rahab and Salmon want to become husband and wife. Had this situation been presented to Moses, and if so, what did he do?

Joshua remembered Moses was challenged by his older sister Miriam and his brother Aaron about his leadership, as he had married a woman outside the covenant people. Zipporah was the daughter of the Midian Priest who worshipped Baal, but then there was the second wife, the Ethiopian (Numbers 12:1–2), two wives who were not covenant women.

Joshua remembered Father God had acted on Moses' behalf and protected him from Miriam's pride threat. Father God's anger burned against Miriam and Aaron for their arrogance, as Miriam was afflicted with leprosy. Aaron pleaded with Moses, asking their sin not be held against them and to ask Father God to heal Miriam, so Moses cried out to Father God to heal her. Father God heard Moses' prayer and instructed Miriam to be confined outside the camp for seven days.

About seven hundred years would pass before Isaiah brought clarification about those who were chosen to join the *"Assembly of the Lord"*, when he wrote:

> *"Also the sons of the foreigner*
> *Who join themselves to the Lord, to serve Him,*
> *And to love the name of the Lord, to be His servants*
> *Everyone who keeps from defiling the Sabbath,*
> *And holds fast My covenant*
> *Even them I will bring to My holy mountain,*
> *And make them joyful in My house of prayer.*
> *Their burnt offerings and their sacrifices*
> *Will be accepted on My altar;*
> *For My house shall be called a house of prayer for all nations."*
> *The Lord God, who gathers the outcasts of Israel, says,*
> *"Yet I will gather to him*
> *Others besides those who are gathered to him."*
>
> Isaiah 56:6–8

For a foreigner to be part of the Assembly, Father God required total allegiance to Him by obeying His commands. This meant a renewing of your mind (Romans 12:2), not being conformed to your old way of life but being renewed in thought, word and deed, through the *"Grace"* of Father God, as He chose you, you did not choose Him.

During the conquest of the southland and the northern conquest, after Joshua allotted to the twelve tribes their inheritance and settled into a life without fighting, Salmon and Rahab were blessed, over time, with three sons. The first was Elimelek, the second remains unnamed, and the third was Boaz.

The Significance of Rahab in Israel's History

Because of her faith, Rahab and her family were spared when Jericho fell (Joshua 6:17, 22–23). But her story didn't end there. She didn't return to her old life; instead, she became part of Israel. Even more astonishing, she became the great-great-grandmother of King David (Matthew 1:5), making her a direct ancestor of Jesus Christ.

The Lord took a woman with a broken past and gave her a legacy of righteousness. This is a beautiful demonstration of how Father God redeemed those who turn to Him, as Rahab's story proves our past does not determine our future when we place our faith in Father God.

Like Rahab, let us choose faith over fear, action over complacency, and Father God over the fleeting securities of this world. When we do, we will find He is faithful to redeem, restore, and give us a future beyond anything we could imagine.

Rahab shows us a core gospel truth: Father God invites us to put our faith in Him, leave our past behind, and join His amazing story of Redemption. Rahab's story demonstrates no one is beyond Father God's love, mercy, or ability to transform their life, which did not disqualify her from Father God's redemptive plan.

While Adam and Eve fell under the curse and sin took hold, Rahab is lifted out of the ashes of Jericho and held up by Father God as a symbol of His *"Grace"*. Father God's choosing of Rahab shows us the fullness of His Redemption and Restoration. Rahab is a picture of Restoration.

Overview

- Rahab's story showcases faith, courage, and redemption in the biblical context.
- Despite her past, she became an ancestor of Jesus Christ.

Who was Rahab?

- Lived in Jericho, a city facing destruction as the Israelites claimed the promised land.
- Not just a prostitute but a high priestess in Baal worship, held in high regard.
- Demonstrated intelligence and discernment about God's power.

Rahab's Journey Begins

- Spies sent by Joshua stayed at Rahab's establishment.
- Rahab hid the spies from the king of Jericho, risking her safety.
- Provided false information to protect them.

Rahab's Confession

- Aware of Israel's history and the fear they instilled in Canaan.
- Acknowledged the Lord as the true God during a meeting with the spies.

Protection

- Made a covenant with the spies to save her family from destruction.
- Tied a scarlet cord in her window as a sign of protection.

Three Days

- Instructed the spies to hide in the mountains for safety.
- Symbolism of three days representing divine intervention.

The Scarlet Cord

- The cord symbolised hope and protection for Rahab and her family.
- Linked to the past when blood was used for protection in Egypt.

Hope Anticipated

- Observed the Israelites marching around Jericho; anxious about the outcome.
- On the seventh day, the front wall of Jericho fell after the Israelites shouted.

Hope Realised

- Rahab and her family were saved by the spies as promised.
- They were integrated into Israelite society and accepted into a new life.

Acceptance

- Rahab married Salmon, raising questions about her acceptance in the community.
- Despite the laws, she was incorporated into the lineage of Israel.

Significance of Rahab in Israel's History

- Rahab's faith led to her family's Salvation and integration into Israel.
- She became an ancestor of King David and Jesus Christ.
- Her life exemplifies Father God's redemptive power over past mistakes.

Ruth

Redemption is often characterised by the generosity of the redeemer, loyalty, and unwavering faithfulness of the receiver, ultimately leading to Restoration and a glorious new future. The Book of Ruth teaches Redemption is possible for the broken and those seen as insignificant. Redemption requires active faith and acceptance, and can be found in unexpected people and circumstances.

Ruth's life serves as an example of Father God's grace extended to a foreign outsider and provides a picture of how Father God redeems individuals from hopeless situations and integrates them into His divine plan. Ruth's restoration included becoming a wife and mother, a mother-in-law, Naomi becoming a grandmother, with their lineage restored, which provided for their future and the community.

A Time to Learn

Ruth belonged to the Moabites, who were related to the Israelites, with both peoples tracing their ancestry back to a common ancestor, Terah, who is named as the father of Abraham and Haran, who was the father of Lot (Genesis 19:30–38). Lot's son, Moab, is described as born from an incestuous relationship between Lot and his eldest daughter after the destruction of Sodom (Genesis 19:37). The Moabites are described as descendants of Lot's son, Moab.

A Time to Understand

The Moabite religion was similar to Baal but with the addition of human sacrifices. Chemosh was the god of the Moabites, who appeared to have a taste for blood. In 2 Kings 3:27, human sacrifice was part of the rites of Chemosh.

This practice, while gruesome, was certainly not unique to the Moabites, as such rites were commonplace in the various Canaanite religious cults, including those of Molech. It should be noted, Numbers 25 records the harlotry the children of Israel took part in, also sacrificing to their gods and bowing down to them.

Only the men of Moab and Amon were forbidden to marry into the Israelite nation, but the women were permitted to convert without restriction. The problem with the Israelites intermarrying with the Moabites, they were drawn away from worshipping the "One True God" into worshipping the gods of the pagans.

A Time to Grieve

There was a famine in Judah, so Elimelech moved his family to Moab, where they could provide for themselves. Ruth the Moabite noticed this family had moved into her village, and observed they were different to all the others she knew.

Ruth and a girlfriend by the name of Orpah became friends with this family of four, the father Elimelech, the mother Naomi, and two sons called Mahlon and Chilion.

Ruth and Orpah were both grieved when the father Elimelech died, leaving Naomi a widow, who cared for her two sons. Not long after the father's death, Mahlon, one of the sons of Naomi, asked Ruth to be his wife, and she consented. Chilion also followed his brother's lead and wed Orpah.

A Time to Mourn

In due course, both of Naomi's sons died, leaving Ruth and Orpah, their wives, childless, living with their mother-in-law, Naomi. Ten years had passed since Elimelech's family first arrived in Moab, and Naomi heard the famine in Judah was over, so she decided to return to Bethlehem.

As Naomi is past the childbearing stage and can offer no solution to her two daughters-in-law for possible husbands, she suggests they return to their respective families. Orpah accepted Naomi's offer, said goodbye and left. Ruth decided to forsake her beliefs and heritage for the God of Naomi, as she said:

> *"Entreat me not to leave you,*
> *or to turn back from following after you;*
> *for wherever you go, I will go;*
> *and wherever you lodge, I will lodge;*

> *Your people shall be my people,*
> *and your God, my God.*
> *Where you die, I will die,*
> *and there will I be buried.*
> *The Lord do so to me and more also,*
> *if anything but death parts you and me."*
>
> Ruth 1:16–17

Ruth was unique, as she was willing to give up her pagan gods for the "One True God". She loved Naomi so much, she was willing to leave her homeland and go to Israel, a land where she would be despised. A mother-in-law's Godly influence over a daughter-in-law, or was it blind faith in someone else's God?

A Time to Plant

Ruth accompanied Naomi to Bethlehem and went to work in the fields gleaning barley, and was soon noticed by Boaz, who took her well-being very seriously as he knew what would happen to a young woman in the fields of other reapers. She was obviously a diligent worker, which would reflect her love and determination to care for Naomi.

Boaz asked his servant who Ruth was. Learning about her background and what she had done for Naomi, he provided protection for her. Boaz instructed his young men to let her glean amongst the sheaves and let grain fall purposely from their bundles for her to gather, and they did. This continued for the whole season of reaping, including the wheat harvest which followed.

A Time to Heal

Boaz lived in Bethlehem, as the scripture says, *"Boaz came from Bethlehem and said to his reapers, 'The Lord be with you!'."* Naomi and Ruth also lived in Bethlehem, for it is written:

> *"Then Ruth took up her barley*
> *and went into the city,*
> *and her mother-in-law*
> *saw what she had gleaned."*

Ruth 2:18

Bethlehem was known as *"The House of Bread"*. Although the word *city* is mentioned, Bethlehem was a relatively small community where everyone knew what everyone did. We know this happened because of what Boaz told Ruth.

> *"It has been fully reported to me,*
> *all that you have done for your mother-in-law*
> *since the death of your husband,*
> *and how you left your father and mother*
> *and the land of your birth,*

and have come to a people
whom you did not know before."

Ruth 2:11

Ruth returned to Naomi with her gleanings of the day and was asked where she had worked (Ruth 2:19). When Ruth replied, the owner of the field was Boaz, Naomi said:

"Blessed be he of the Lord,
who has not forsaken His kindness
to the living and the dead!
This man is a relation of ours,
one of our close relatives."

Ruth 2:20

Ruth had no understanding of the Israelites' customs and obligations, but trusted Naomi to teach and lead her in the ways of the Israelites. With the passing of time, after Naomi assured Ruth she had her best interests at heart, instructed Ruth to wash, anoint herself and dress in her best clothes, then go down to the threshing floor of Boaz.

Naomi told Ruth to make sure she was not seen but to wait until after Boaz had eaten and lay down to sleep. Naomi said:

> *"When he is asleep, go in,*
> *uncover his feet, and lie down;*
> *and he will tell you what you should do."*
> *Ruth replied,*
> *"All that you say to me I will do."*

Ruth 3:4–5

Now it happened at midnight that the man was startled, and turned himself; and there, a woman was lying at his feet. And he said, "Who are you?" So she answered, "I am Ruth, your maidservant. Take your maidservant under your wing, for you are a close relative." Ruth 3:8–9

Boaz replied:

> *"Blessed are you of the Lord, my daughter!*
> *For you have shown more kindness*
> *at the end than at the beginning,*
> *in that you did not go after young men,*
> *whether poor or rich."*

Ruth 3:10

Boaz continued:

> *"And now, my daughter, do not fear.*
> *I will do for you all that you request,*
> *for all the people of my town*
> *know that you are a virtuous woman."*

Ruth 3:11

A Time to Reap

Boaz was a "Kinsman Redeemer", meaning he was a male relative who had the responsibility to help a relative in need or danger. Naomi and, in particular, Ruth, both fell into this category, as Naomi's husband and both sons, one of whom was the husband of Ruth, died, leaving the women penniless and without a male protector.

The question to be asked is, "What was expected of a 'Kinsman Redeemer'?"

- Redeeming and restoring a family member's lost property.
- Ensuring family continuity and justice.
- Paying any accumulated debts.
- Marrying a childless widow to continue the deceased husband's line.

A Time to Embrace

Through a series of events, directed by Naomi and the obedience of Ruth, Boaz sought to take Ruth as his wife, but there was a closer relative who was entitled to care for Elimelech's family.

When Boaz presented him with all the facts, this relative claimed, due to an issue with his inheritance, he could not redeem a Moabite. This was so different to his father Salmon, who married Rahab and cared for her family, as they were part of the tribe of Judah so many years previously.

Salmon had three sons: the first was Elimelech, the second was unnamed, and the third was Boaz. As the eldest son, Elimelech received the major share of his father's inheritance, which now belonged to Naomi, whose first son, Mahlon, inherited the major share from his father. Because both sons had died, the inheritance reverted to Naomi.

Boaz was well aware of the Deuteronomic law regarding the "Duty of the surviving brother" (Deuteronomy 25:5-10), and this he carried out, not only redeeming Naomi and her deceased husband's land, but also her daughter-in-law, Ruth, whom he was able to take as wife. As Boaz had redeemed both, he received the major share of his father's property as an addition to his own inheritance, which blessed him further.

A Time to Keep

After Boaz finalised some family details, he took Ruth to be his wife. Boaz was under a binding obligation to raise a family on behalf of his dead relative. Failing to do this was to place a person under grave reprehension by God and liable to punishment.

As Boaz sat at the town gate, a place where legal matters and issues of civil counsel took place, he called ten of the elders to be his witnesses in acquiring the land from Naomi and the right to marry Ruth, his older deceased brother's daughter-in-law. The people who were at the gate, and the elders, said:

> *"We are witnesses.*
> *The Lord make the woman*
> *who is coming to your house like Rachel and Leah,*
> *the two who built the house of Israel;*
> *and may you prosper in Ephrathah*
> *and be famous in Bethlehem.*
> *May your house be like the house of Perez,*
> *whom Tamar bore to Judah,*
> *because of the offspring which the Lord*
> *will give you from this young woman."*

Ruth 4:11–12

Boaz redeemed Ruth by acting as her "Kinsman Redeemer", a legal role in ancient Israel. After the nearest relative declined to marry Ruth and maintain Naomi's family inheritance, Boaz stepped in. He publicly sealed the transaction in the town gate before the elders, acquiring Naomi's land and taking Ruth as his wife to continue the deceased husband's name and legacy.

A Time to Love

Boaz took on the responsibility, which was a voluntary act of kindness and honour, not a strict obligation. Boaz and Ruth married and had a son named Obed, who was the grandfather of King David and an ancestor of Jesus, securing the family line. Naomi's poverty was transformed into joy as she gained a grandson and was provided for through Boaz's honourable actions.

A Time to Speak

Reading the story of Naomi, Ruth, and Boaz raises the question, "Who was the true redeemer?" Boaz is explicitly called a "Kinsman Redeemer" in Ruth 2:20, and he gathered witnesses when he officially took on that role. The likelihood of his ability to provide for Ruth for the rest of her life, given his redemption was likely for a short time, as he was much older than Ruth, can Boaz be considered the "true" redeemer?

In a sense, Ruth served as a redeemer. Naomi is a destitute widow, bitter and living in a foreign land, when she decided to return to Bethlehem. Ruth refused to stay in Moab, choosing to go to Judea instead. The fact that Ruth *"clung"* to Naomi makes her a candidate for being the story's "true" redeemer. Were it not for Ruth's faithfulness, Naomi may never have been redeemed.

Obed, the son of Boaz and Ruth, could also be the "true" redeemer. The women of the city identified Obed as Naomi's redeemer (Ruth 4:14). After the death of Boaz, Obed was the one to care for Naomi and Ruth in their old age; he was a more "permanent" redeemer than Boaz could have been. Obed was the grandfather of David, through whom the Redeemer of the world would come, and it is the mention of David at the narrative's end, gives the whole story its significance.

We know the Lord God is the ultimate Redeemer, as we see Father God's hand working behind the scenes throughout the book of Ruth:

- Father God sent the famine that drove Naomi's family to Moab, where Ruth was. Ruth 1:1
- Father God made certain Ruth "happened" to come to the field of Boaz. Ruth 2:3
- Father God had previously instituted the law of levirate marriage. Deuteronomy 25:5–6; Ruth 4:5
- Father God enabled Ruth to conceive. Ruth 4:13

Through it all, Father God planned to bring King David into the world and continue the bloodline of Christ. Ruth 4:17–22

A Time to Reflect and Reveal

A drought was in full swing, so Elimelech, along with Naomi and his two sons, left their home and property, his inheritance from Salmon and Rahab and lived in the land of Moab. Elimelech eventually died, leaving his two sons to provide for their mother, Naomi.

The two sons married, but they also died, leaving both their wives childless. As the two wives loved Naomi, they supported her during this time when they all shared a common view as widows.

Naomi, after the two sons had passed away, should have returned to Bethlehem and gone to the next brother, as he was responsible for providing sons for her two daughters-in-law.

But Naomi stayed in Moab for ten years until she, by her own confession, was too old to have any more children (Ruth 1:11). When Naomi heard that the famine was over in Bethlehem, she devised a plan to return to her home, sell the land, the inheritance her husband had received.

This plan fell apart to some extent when Ruth chose to remain with her. As Naomi could not convince Ruth otherwise, she stopped trying to persuade her (Ruth 1:18). On their return, Ruth continued to provide for her mother-in-law, Naomi.

Under Deuteronomic Law (Deuteronomy 25:5–10), Naomi should now approach the next brother about providing another child for her to carry on the eldest son's family bloodline, but because she was beyond childbearing age and had a daughter-in-law, this did not happen.

It was Naomi's responsibility, once the brother refused to marry, to take his sandal and give it to the brother in front of the elders and spit in his face (Deuteronomy 25:9), but this did not happen.

When Naomi saw how the youngest brother, Boaz, cared for Ruth, she came up with an alternative plan for survival, which involved Ruth. After Naomi told Ruth what she was about to ask her to do was all about seeking security for her, Ruth replied:

> *"All that you say to me*
>
> *I will do."*

Ruth 3:5

Although some hesitancy could be noticed in her reply, because Ruth loved Naomi, she did all Naomi instructed her to do. Whether Ruth totally understood the implications is unknown, as she was obedient in all her ways.

Boaz took the part that Naomi should have fulfilled and met with his older brother. When the older brother refused to redeem the land Naomi was selling, Boaz presented him with the sandal, but did not spit in his face.

Naomi was bitter when she returned, as she instructed the other women to call her Mara, not Naomi (Ruth 1:20). Through Ruth's acceptance of all Naomi's instructions, Naomi was redeemed and blessed as Ruth conceived and had a son, whom they called Obed.

Although the plan that Naomi devised was flawed with problems, Father God steered a course through all the twists and turns, instigated by His plan, will and purpose.

> *"A man's heart plans his way,*
> *but the Lord directs his steps."*
>
> Proverbs 16:9

In this story of sadness and lack of trust, Father God had a plan for the continuance of His ordained bloodline. The parable of the Prodigal Son can also be seen as a parallel to some extent, but it was the wife who finally came to her senses and returned home to find Father God had provided for her in so many unexpected ways.

A Time to Review

This text is a summary and exploration of the Book of Ruth, highlighting its themes of Redemption, Faith, and Restoration.

Redemption Theme:

- Ruth, a Moabite, becomes part of Father God's plan through faith and loyalty.
- Redemption is shown as possible for outsiders and the seemingly insignificant.

Moabite Background:

- Ruth descends from Moab, tracing back to Lot through a complicated family history.
- Moabites practised a different, harsher religion, including human sacrifice.

Ruth Meets Naomi's Family:

- Naomi, her husband Elimelech, and their sons moved to Moab due to famine.
- Ruth marries Mahlon; Naomi, Ruth, and Orpah are all widowed.

Loyalty and Leave:

- Naomi returns to Bethlehem; Ruth insists on staying with her, declaring full loyalty and adopting Naomi's God.
- Orpah returns to her family; Ruth leaves her homeland and culture.

Life in Bethlehem:

- Ruth supports Naomi by gleaning in fields, attracting Boaz's attention for her diligence and loyalty.
- Boaz, a relative, protects Ruth and ensures she gathers enough food.

The Role of the Kinsman Redeemer:

- Boaz, as "Kinsman Redeemer", legally redeems Naomi's land and takes Ruth as wife to preserve the family lineage.
- The nearest relative relinquishes the right; Boaz marries Ruth in a public legal transaction.

Restoration and Legacy:

- Ruth and Boaz have a son, Obed, King David's grandfather and ancestor of Jesus.
- Naomi's fortunes are restored, securing the family's future.

Ultimate Redeemer Question:

- The text discusses whether Boaz, Ruth, or Obed is the true earthly redeemer.
- Father God is shown orchestrating events behind the scenes, emphasising divine redemption and providence.

Jonah and Peter

When researching the content of *Redeemed*, it became evident two people had similar experiences in Father God's redemptive plan. Their journey is described:

> *"No temptation has overtaken you*
> *except such as is common to man;*
> *but God is faithful,*
> *who will not allow you to be tempted*
> *beyond what you are able,*
> *but with the temptation*
> *will also make the way of escape,*
> *that you may be able to bear it."*
>
> 1 Corinthians 10:13

Although many years separated Jonah and Peter, there are a number of similarities between them as they were called to complete a mission ordained by Father God.

Jonah lived in Gath Hepher, near Nazareth, and Peter lived in Capernaum; each village was situated in Galilee. Both were

Galileans, and so were their personalities. A Galilean is described as more anxious for honour than gain, quick-tempered, impulsive, emotional, easily roused by an appeal to adventure, but loyal to the end.

John recorded in his Gospel, when Jesus was addressing Peter as *the son of Jonah*, said:

> *"He (Andrew) brought him (Peter) to Jesus.*
> *Now when Jesus looked at him, He said,*
> *'You are Simon the son of Jonah.*
> *You shall be called Cephas'*
> *which is translated, A Stone."*

John 1:42

Reference to Jonah is mentioned because Peter's father's name was Jonah (Strong's 2495). In biblical times, a person's name was significant, often reflecting their character, role, or origin and could be changed by Father God to signify a new path in their life. As the callings of Jonah and Peter are considered, what similarities are evident in their lives?

Similarities between Jonah and Peter

- Neither was perfect in how they served Father God.
- Both refused the first call to minister.
- Both accepted the second call.

- Both experienced miracles.
- Both wanted Father God to leave them alone.
- Both faced a crisis during a storm.
- Both were peacemakers.
    a. Jonah to the Ninevites.
    b. Peter, after his confession, "Jesus was the Christ."
- Neither experienced patience.
    a. Jonah and the outcome of Nineveh.
    b. Peter going fishing at Capernium.
- Both received a second chance to submit to their calling.
- Both sought forgiveness after diverse circumstances.
- Both were first to cross Jew/Gentile boundaries.
- Both went to Joppa.
    a. Jonah fled from Joppa to avoid going to the Gentiles.
    b. Peter went to Joppa in Acts 10:5–6.

The biblical comparison between Peter and Jonah can be explored through their shared connection to the sea and their reluctance to engage with Gentiles. While Jonah ran from God's command to preach to the Gentiles, Peter, after initial denial, ultimately became a key figure in spreading the gospel to non-Jews, fulfilling a similar but opposite mission.

The main difference between the two men is, Jonah was a prophet who fled from God's instructions, while Peter was an apostle, despite his initial impulsive tendencies, ultimately obeyed and expanded the mission of Father God to the

Gentiles. Both were called by the Father and had significant, though different, experiences with the sea and a mission to non-Jews, but their responses to their divine callings ultimately set them apart.

The difference between Jonah and Peter

- Jonah remained stubborn and rebellious.
- Peter went from rebellion to complete submission and firm belief.

Jonah only experienced one recorded sea encounter, whereas Peter, a fisherman, knew the sea well. Jonah's story took place in the open sea, where Peter's stories were all contained in the Sea of Galilee and Tiberias. Peter's encounters were different to Jonah's; as Jonah disobeyed Father God, Peter was reliant on His Son, Jesus, for protection and guidance.

Peter's encounters with the sea

- Sea of Galilee. One net was used when Jesus said two to catch the fish. Luke 5:4–7
- Sea of Galilee. Wind and waves obeyed Jesus. Matthew 8:23–27
- Sea of Galilee. Walked on water to Jesus, but faith failed. Matthew 14:28–31
- Sea of Tiberias. Caught a fish with a coin in its mouth. Matthew 17:27
- Sea of Tiberias. Failed to walk on water as joy turned to despair and misery. John 21:7–11

Jonah and Peter

Jonah and Peter, though separated by time, share notable similarities in their callings and responses to Father God, yet have key differences in their behaviour and outcomes. Jonah was stubborn and ran from Father God's demands; Peter moved from denial to foundational obedience. Jonah's only sea encounter was his voyage, while Peter had many, usually on the Sea of Galilee or Tiberias. Peter's reliance was on Jesus during his sea experiences, unlike Jonah.

Jonah lived under the Law, where Peter went from Law to Grace, accompanied by the power of the Holy Spirit. Jonah knew Father God was feared, but experienced personally the mercy He gave when His will was obeyed. Peter feared Father God until the infilling of the Holy Spirit changed him completely, as he became Father God's servant, choosing to obey the known will of the Father to all those who were led into his ministry.

I'VE BEEN REDEEMED

1 *I've been redeemed (I've been redeemed)
by the blood of the Lamb. (by the blood of the Lamb.)
I've been redeemed (I've been redeemed)
by the blood of the Lamb,
I've been redeemed by the blood of the Lamb,
saved and sanctified I am.
All my sins are washed away,
I've been redeemed.*

2 *I've been redeemed (I've been redeemed)
by the blood of the Lamb. (by the blood of the Lamb.)
I've been redeemed (I've been redeemed)
by the blood of the Lamb,
I've been redeemed by the blood of the Lamb,
filled with the Holy Ghost I am.
All my sins are washed away,
I've been redeemed.*

3 *I've been redeemed (I've been redeemed)
by the blood of the Lamb. (by the blood of the Lamb.)
I've been redeemed (I've been redeemed)
by the blood of the Lamb,
I've been redeemed by the blood of the Lamb,
oh, and I praise God I am.
All my sins are washed away,
I've been redeemed.*

Redeemed

4 *And that's not all; (and that's not all;)*
there's more besides. (there's more besides.)
No, that's not all; (No, that's not all;)
there's more besides.
No, that's not all; there's more besides.
I've been to the river,
and I've been baptised.
All my sins are washed away,
I've been redeemed.

5 *He's coming back (He's coming back)*
to take me home. (to take me home.)
He's coming back (He's coming back)
to take me home. (to take me home.)
He's coming back to take me home.
I'll shout "Hallelujah" before His throne.
All my sins are washed away;
I've been redeemed.

6 *It's by God's grace (it's by God's grace)*
that I've been saved. (that I've been saved.)
It's by God's grace (it's by God's grace)
that I've been saved. (that I've been saved.)
It's by God's grace that I've been saved.
I have no fear on the Judgment Day.
All my sins are washed away;
I've been redeemed.

Anonymous

OTHER BOOKS BY THE AUTHOR

Available from www.wittonbooks.com

The four Gospels and the first two chapters of Acts, using the NKJ Version, have been chronologically ordered and then blended to form a single, cohesive narrative.

The four Gospels and the first two chapters of Acts, using the NIV, have been chronologically ordered and then blended to form a cohesive story.

The Birth of Jesus is retold, as many accepted truths are distorted facts. Retelling the true story brings many hidden truths to the surface.

Available from www.wittonbooks.com

This book covers several mysteries, including the *"Trinity"* and the End Times.

The roads taken by several Bible characters and the consequences of their chosen walks.

Many of those in the Bible who were betrayed in life are investigated to gain the real meaning behind their betrayal.

Each promise given to Abram is researched through the lives of Moses and Joshua, with further insights into the lives of the children of Israel.

Available from www.wittonbooks.com

This is a sequel to the previous book, but it explores other parts not previously covered.

Paul, when writing his last letter to Timothy, said that his life had been *poured out as a drink offering*. Discover the meaning of the *drink offering* and how the offering applies to the *Called*.

Those who hear "Well done, good and faithful" will experience a transformation in body, soul and spirit. The Bible provides us with glimpses into what the eternal future holds for the faithful.

Available from www.wittonbooks.com
and *The Adventures of Max* Facebook page

Series titles available:

Book 1	*The Defiant Mouse*
Book 2	*The Curious Chicken*
Book 3	*A Dog in Need*
Book 4	*An Old Friend Found*
Book 5	*The Rescue*
Book 6	*The Bush Fire*
Book 7	*A Bad Influence*
Book 8	*A Shining Light*
Book 9	*Hidden Secrets*
Book 10	*A Foiled Plot*
Book 11	*Running the Race*
Book 12	*An Unexpected Reward*
Book 13	*Max Meets a Friend*
Book 14	*Reflections*

**Available from www.wittonbooks.com
and *Manuel's Missions* Facebook page**

Series titles available:

Book 1	*The Servant Mouse*
Book 2	*A Cherished Place*
Book 3	*Manuel and the Spider*
Book 4	*A Generous Giver*
Book 5	*Lost and Found*
Book 6	*Manuel's Day Out*
Book 7	*Love One Another*
Book 8	*Observations*

www.ingramcontent.com/pod-product-compliance
Lightning Source LLC
Chambersburg PA
CBHW062031290426
44109CB00026B/2596